Birth of a Bookworm

Michel Tremblay

translated by Sheila Fischman

Talonbooks

2003

Talonbooks
P.O. Box 2076, Vancouver, British Columbia, Canada V6B 3S3
www.talonbooks.com

Typeset in Scala and printed and bound in Canada.

First Printing: June 2003

First published in French in 1994 as *Un ange cornu avec des ailes de tôle*
by Les Editions Leméac, Montreal.

National Library of Canada Cataloguing in Publication Data
Tremblay, Michel, 1942–
    [Ange cornu avec des ailes de tôle. English]
    Birth of a bookworm / Michel Tremblay ; translated by Sheila Fischman

    Translation of: Un ange cornu avec des ailes de tôle.
    ISBN 0-88922-476-5

    1. Tremblay, Michel, 1942– —Childhood and youth. 2. Authors,
Canadian (French)—20th century—Biography. 3. Books and reading. I.
Fischman, Sheila. II. Title.
PS8539.R47A8413 2003   C843'.54   C2003-910125-8
PQ3919.2.T73A8413 2003

The publisher gratefully acknowledges the financial support of the
Canada Council for the Arts; the Government of Canada through the
Book Publishing Industry Development Program; and the Province of
British Columbia through the British Columbia Arts Council for our
publishing activities.

For François Mercier, who always comes up with words to encourage me whenever I have doubts.
—M.T.

This translation is for Bill Glassco.
—S.F.

No one can tell a story exactly the way it happened. You clean it up. You try to recapture the original emotion. Till what you're left with is nostalgia. And if there's one thing that's a long way from the truth, it's nostalgia. And so it's not your story.
— Dany Laferrière

I am certain of nothing but the holiness of the heart's affections and the truth of imagination.
— John Keats

By Way of Introduction

Do you, like me, dream in the style of the author you've been reading before you fall asleep? If so, mount this *joual*, this horse of mine, as late at night as possible, take off with him while you sleep, he's friskier than ever in spite of all the uptight supporters of the "there's-just-one-way-to-write-proper-French" crowd, he's pawing the ground with impatience while he waits, and I promise you, he gallops like a god! You see, I'd like to be able to think that I too have the ability to make you dream.

— M. T.

My mother's roots are complicated and mysterious. Born in Providence, Rhode Island, to Maria Desrosiers, a Cree from Saskatoon who spoke French, but badly, and a sailor from Brittany by the name of Rathier, whose first name I never knew and who soon disappeared into the abyss of memory, she was brought up by her maternal grandmother because Maria Desrosiers-Rathier had decided to stay in the States, to work there, according to some family members, to live a life of debauchery, according to others, and because her children got in her way. So she'd put them on the train and stayed in Providence where it must have been easier to find money than it was in the Middle of Nowhere, Saskatchewan.

How did my mother end up coming to Montreal in the early 1920s to marry my father? I don't know. I could call and ask one of my brothers but I'd rather believe in the call of destiny, the inevitability of fate, and some incredible adventures back and forth across America twice in search of love and happiness ... I'm a child of Jules Verne, of Victor Malo and Raoul de Navery, and I've always assumed that I had a mother straight out of an adventure story.

As a child, I would try to imagine what my mother's life would have been like if she hadn't left Saskatchewan. Whom would she have married? *And who would have been my father?* And when I learned that it takes two to make a child, that if they hadn't met I wouldn't have existed, I had my first existential crisis. So chance plays an important part in making babies, does it? And if my mother had stayed in Saskatchewan, my father would have met some other woman and I wouldn't have been there wondering why they hadn't met? I nearly hadn't been born and nobody seemed to care.

Saskatchewan was always floating around in the apartment on Fabre Street and then the one on Cartier, a tremendous ghost the colour of ripe wheat and a too-blue sky. When Mama talked about the prairie that had no beginning and no end, about the fantastic sunsets above a sea of wheat, the brushfires that spread at the speed of a galloping horse, about the horses too, in fact, that she'd loved so much, always with a little quaver in her voice and her gaze turned to the window to hide the homesickness that made her eyes mist over, I wished that I could board the train—the long one that took five days to travel all the way across Canada—and take her to the middle of an endless field lulled by the south wind and the cry of the mourning dove, and tell her: "Breathe, look, touch, devour this landscape; it's my gift to you."

My father, a good man but of whom diplomacy was not the principal virtue, often promised when he was drinking, because he loved her, that he *really* would take her one last time to her native land, which was even farther away than that of Gabrielle Roy, whose books she consumed with long painful sighs. She had one brief moment of hope, but she knew as well as the rest of us that she would be forever a prisoner of Montreal where her wandering had brought her for good, and she'd fall back into those endless reveries she'd share with us in little bits and tiny scraps. I would climb onto her huge, soft, fragrant body, throw myself onto what I used to call her two pillows because I'd often fell asleep there, and I'd say: "Katchewan!" The floodgates of memory would open, the two of us would glide onto a river of melancholy for her, plans for western journeys for me.

I've never been to Saskatchewan, and fields that are too flat, too vast, too lulled by the wind break my heart.

***

Did Mama have an English accent? Today I ask myself that question before I talk about her sister, my Aunt Bea who, like her mother, Maria Desrosiers, whom I never really knew, didn't speak French very well. Could my mother have had an English accent without our realizing it? Can a person spend the first twenty years of his life in the company of someone who has a foreign accent and not know it? That's something I checked with my brothers: whew!

My mother and my Aunt Bea (with no acute accent and it was her full name, not a diminutive for Beatrice) could have been twins, they resembled each other so much: the same vast frame, broad but not tall, the same square face, the same round cheeks, the same long, flat forehead scored very early with deep wrinkles, the same copper-coloured skin—and the infectious Desrosiers smile that as soon as it appeared, wiped out all your anxieties and troubles. The spitting image of their mother. They'd inherited nothing from the Breton sailor, whose only role had been to conceive them, and everything from the resourceful Cree woman who had crossed half a continent in an attempt to earn some kind of living in the land of opportunity. All she'd brought with her though were three daughters and a son who all resembled her.

When the two went walking along Mont-Royal Street, speaking English to be sure that their secrets, the secrets of two little girls who hadn't grown up, stayed secret, people would say:

"Madame Tremblay's happy today, her twin sister's come for a visit!"

They kept telling each other the same stories about their far-off childhood in the depths of Saskatchewan: Aunt Bea, who always kept a few peanuts in her purse on Sunday afternoon so she could boast about finishing her snack *after* her sister; the rages of my already greedy mother, who would salivate at the sight of her older sister eating even the peanut shells to stretch out her own enjoyment and to sharpen her sister's frustration; the nuns who made them repeat the same French phrases hundreds and hundreds of times in an attempt to correct their pronunciation, because at home, English was the dominant language; the famous time—this I've heard before, followed by Mama's loud laugh and her compassionate tears in the face of a mistake made by a little girl who wanted to do the right thing—when my mother had stood up straight and proud in the classroom to recite her lesson but in her nervousness had confused two phrases in the exercise and had confidently declared: "Red as a banana!"; the brush fires that constantly recurred in the Desrosiers' conversations: the raw, uncontrollable terror, the smell of burnt grass, the smoke that caught in your throat, the maddened animals, the children and their grandmother clinging together in a pond while they waited for the volunteer firemen ... Little girls of fifty, pursuing a conversation started four decades earlier and careful never to end it.

They didn't see each other very often and whenever one of them visited the other, it was a feast. A feast of confidences exchanged over a cup of green tea (my Grandmother Tremblay always called it "Indian tea" because it was provided by our maternal grandmother and for some unknown reason was always served on grand occasions); loud laughter soon followed by tears, especially those of Aunt Bea whose husband, Arthur Liasse, neglected her shamelessly; consolations and advice murmured half in English, half in French, heads together and handkerchiefs shared. When Aunt Bea left, my mother would slip a bill into her hand or her purse.

"Please don't do that," she'd whisper in English. "You don't have to, Rhéauna ... I'm the oldest, I should be giving you money ... "

"Take it. You need it more than I do ... And keep your voice down, Michel's probably listening ... "

Hearing my name, I pricked up my ears. Too late ...

***

I'm lying on my back. Reading. Like every night before I go to sleep. Because Aunt Bea was there, we'd watched "I Love Lucy" on TV instead of "Les Belles histoires des pays d'en haut." Which meant that it was a Monday night in winter. At half-past eight my mother gestures to me to go to my bedroom, a double room looking on the corner of Mont-Royal and Cartier that I share with my two older brothers. I realized that Aunt Bea had something to tell her so I left with my book, not making too big a fuss.

But I can't concentrate, even though the book is fascinating—Le Château des Carpates, by Jules Verne, or a novel by Captain W.E. Johns; a big fat decrepit volume, all soft and smelling of dust, that I'd borrowed from the municipal library across the street from Parc Lafontaine. I followed my usual ritual: I sat on the edge of the convertible sofa that served as my bed, held the book against my chest after letting its odour seep into me, said a quick prayer, not to God but to the joy of reading—so strong, so powerful—that I was so afraid of losing when I got old (I'm maybe ten at the time and naively haunted by the thought that some day I'll be blasé because I'll have read everything, so I pray for my joy to remain complete until I die and for the authors of books to go on writing!), then I stretched out on my back with the pillow folded under my neck. The pleasure of opening the book, of cracking the spine, of checking to see how many pages are left to read ... That night though, nothing doing: the murmurs, the unsuccessfully suppressed shouts from the dining room, where two cups of green tea are steaming, keep me from concentrating on the adventures of Jules Verne's hero, Franz de Telek, or Worrals, the Captain Johns heroine I like so much, because she's a woman, an aviatrix who's as good at outsmarting the evil Nazis as her companions, Biggles and King, whom I find a little boring, with their over-confident male arrogance (I haven't fallen in love with King yet). At least Worrals sometimes admits that she's scared!

Bits of conversation come to me after they've travelled across the house, some words that I understand, others, in English, whose meaning I try to guess, whose weight I try to judge because they're spoken with such distress. I think they've cried a little and I lean my head and shoulders out of bed with one hand resting on the floor. But I can't hear any better and my wrist quickly goes numb. I consider getting up quietly, walking down the corridor, and hiding in the tiny storage area in one corner of the kitchen, but the floor creaks, and the last time we had company, I'd paid the consequences.

"Go back to bed you little snoop and don't listen in on adults! You wouldn't understand what we're talking about anyway! He's such a brat, always sticking his nose where it doesn't belong!"

I try to get involved in my book again. Sounds from the kitchen. Cups and saucers clinking, a purse opening, a nose being blown, the purse closed again. The click of metal on metal. Aunt Bea is leaving. I know what comes next, it's the same every time, and I decide I'll pretend to be asleep so I won't have to suffer the damp assaults of my mother's "twin" who smells a little too much like Auntie Clean for my liking ... But I don't have time to switch off the light; they're already in the corridor that leads to my room.

"He's already asleep ... with a book on his chest ... Isn't that cute ... "

"That's what you think ... He's going to wear his eyes out with that foolishness ... "

My mother's tone is unmistakable: she knows perfectly well that I'm not asleep and she wants me to know that she's not taken in by my little game. They keep switching back between English and French.

"*You can't say he reads too much* ... You're the one that encourages him to read ... "

"I tell him not to bend his neck when he's reading, not to read lying down but to sit up straight, make sure there's enough light and that it comes from the left and to turn it off before he goes to sleep ... But does he listen? He never listens now ... "

"*Don't say that, he looks so sweet ...* "

"Oh sure, *he looks so sweet* when there's people around, but he's on another planet when I'm alone with him!"

"I'm sure you're exaggerating ... "

Then comes the punishment. She does it on purpose, I know she does.

"Okay, kiss him goodnight before you go, otherwise I'll get mad and *that* will wake him up!"

Horrors! A mass that's both solid and soft bends over me, a perfume that may have gone bad fills my nostrils, a big fat wet kiss smears my cheek. I can't put my hand up to wipe it off, I have to stay absolutely still, my mother knows that perfectly well and I can sense her snickering to herself. I could pretend to wake up, smile at my aunt, turn to face the wall as I pull up the covers, but I decide to play the game all the way and I lie there in my bed totally inert, a dead weight. She won't win, she won't make me act out a scene I'm not sure I could do properly, she'll never know whether I'm sleeping or not.

"*You were lucky with your last child, Rhéauna. He looks like an angel!*"

"Sure. An angel with horns. And tin wings!"

L'AUBERGE DE L'ANGE-GARDIEN (Angel Inn)

The Comtesse de Ségur

According to family legend, from my earliest childhood I could be seen walking through the house clutching a book to my chest. Now, legends have their own way of interpreting facts that may be very unimportant, and that one is a powerful example: from the age of two or three I walked around the house clutching a book to my chest quite simply because I was my Grandmother Tremblay's delivery boy.

Olivine Tremblay (who was born Tremblay, as it happens, at Les Éboulements, and never shed her lovely Charlevoix County accent) was an inveterate reader who would read anything—Balzac and Bordeaux, Zola and Zévaco, without distinction, without contempt for some and with damp admiration for others—for the story that was told between the covers and most of all, I think, for the hours of escape given her by the books she borrowed from the library. She'd raised too many children for her liking—seven, I think—and she let them raise their own without getting too involved. By living, I suppose, through books from France, the great adventures that she hadn't been allowed.

Settled discreetly in her rocking chair in one corner of the dining room, she would disappear with obvious pleasure into the Guermantes' salon or the bell towers of Notre-Dame-de-Paris, wetting her thumb to turn the pages, sometimes closing her eyes at the end of a chapter she'd particularly liked. I'll never forget the day when, deep in the *Vicomte de Bargelonne*, she started snickering when she read that one of the villains in the novel, the governor of the Bastille prison, was a Tremblay.

"There's one Tremblay that stayed in France, Nana! A bandit, no less! And then governor of the Bastille! Finally, a Tremblay that did something with his life!"

She and my mother had a good laugh and I never understood why.

She was very old when I knew her, already past sixty when I was born, and she scared me a little because of her limp. I would hear her get up every morning, when we were living on Fabre Street, and the sound she made as she travelled the long corridor from her bedroom to the kitchen haunted my last moments of sleep: a heavy footfall, a leg gliding along the floor ... (When my father heard his mother walk, he'd say with a wink: "One yes, one no; one yes; one no ... ") Later on, when I read *Treasure Island*, I immediately associated Long John Silver's way of walking with my grandmother's, and it was she, with a black patch over one eye and a hand-carved wooden leg, who terrorized the poor hero of the novel. I called the pirate "Long John Silvette" to make him less scary ...

She liked to read then but she was rather forgetful and often left her book in her bedroom.

"Michel, sweetheart, would you go to gramma's room and get her book?"

And strangely enough she often forgot her book *in the evening* when it was very dark ...

"I think gramma dropped it on the floor, dear ... Maybe it's under the bed! Take a good look and don't come back and say it isn't there, because it is!"

It's hard for me to describe the terror of those brief moments spent in my grandmother's pitch-black bedroom, looking for an open book on the kitchen chair that served as her bedside table or on the floor near the bed where dusteroos—those accumulations of dust my brothers claimed were potential monsters that were born under beds so they could bite little children's toes—were liable to jump on me at any moment ... It was a pure, white terror that still makes me shiver when I think about it. If I ran into one of my brothers in the corridor, he would ask: "Are you going to gramma's bedroom?" and roll his eyes ... If I got out of that damn room with the damn book pressed against me, it wasn't from a precocious love of literature (I was too young even to know the meaning of "read"), but because I was so scared, I clung to the only tangible thing I could get my hands on ... Actually, it's amazing that it didn't turn me off reading for good.

On Fabre Street what also helped to spread the legend of the-little-boy-who-dreamed-very-young-of-learning-how-to-read was the fact that across from us lived a Madame Allard, who was crippled like my grandmother and was also an avid reader of anything readable, trading with my grandmother the books that she'd borrowed from the Immaculée-Conception parish library. Each was allowed three books every two weeks which meant that they both read six, counting the ones I delivered as soon as they were read.

"Gramma finished this book last night, dear. Will you take it over to Madame Allard and ask her for one that she's finished?"

(It's weird the way Quebeckers talk about themselves in the third person when they speak to children, as if they don't really exist: "Mama doesn't want you to do that," Or, "Papa wants to know if you were a good boy today," or "Come and see Uncle, he's got a nice surprise for you," or "Come and give Auntie a kiss.")

And so I crossed the street every other day, clutching a book to my chest, while in the summer the neighbours looked on and jumped to the wrong conclusion.

One last thing before we leave, my grandmother reading in front of the huge radio that was always tuned to the soap operas on Radio-Canada or CKAC, the only things, according to my mother, that could make her take her nose out of her books: she never talked to Madame Allard though she traded books with her for years! As they were both crippled, they never went out and I suppose they never felt a need to communicate by phone. In the summer, my grandmother sometimes sat out on the balcony with a 7-Up, which she adored, and watched me cross the street with a novel I was going to deliver to her friend whom she didn't know. Madame Allard would be on her balcony, too. The two of them might wave or nod a greeting, but that was all. They'd never ask, "Did you like the book?" nor would they say, "You'll love this one, it's really sad," no, most likely they knew that they both loved anything that could be read and that any criticism or appreciation would be superfluous.

During this time I got used to holding books against my chest. Even now, at the age of fifty-one, particularly if a book is heavy, I still catch myself almost automatically holding it that way, like a tic, and when I do, I have an inner smile for Olivine Tremblay, who taught me how to walk on the street holding against my heart all the knowledge in the world.

***

The very first book I ever read was *L'Auberge de l'Ange-Gardien*, by the Comtesse de Ségur, and it was quite an adventure.

I was seven or eight years old, I'd been acting as an intermediary between my grandmother and our neighbour across the street for several years, and I was beginning to wonder seriously what there could be in those big books with no pictures that was so fascinating for two old ladies, they spent days at a time with them. I had my own books, but they were full of big coloured illustrations and the stories in them were short and printed in big letters, while the dusty volumes with grey or brown covers that I transported had pages yellowed and stained from use, tiny print that discouraged reading, and not even one little drawing that could help you out if you didn't really understand everything in them. But I adored the way they smelled and I was always rubbing my nose against them.

One afternoon in December I saw my father standing watch outside my parents' bedroom and I thought: "Oh boy, it'll soon be Christmas and Mama's hiding the presents." She always hid them at the back of her closet because she knew I was afraid of the millions and billions of monsters that hid in it and would never, ever go hunting there ... But I was getting older and the stories that my brothers and my girl-cousins told me, so useful for keeping me quiet when I was really little, were getting stale ... For a while now I'd suspected that our closets were too small to be hiding places for King Kong, the wicked witch in *Snow White*, and the Devil himself in person with his court of foul-mouthed, cloven-hooved demons and his complete set of instruments of torture. One in each closet maybe ... But *all* of them in *every* closet? For pete's sake, who did they think they were kidding?

And so the next Saturday morning, the time my mother had chosen to do her week's grocery shopping at Monsieur Soucis'—she pronounced it "Soucisse," like sausage and never dared to ask if he had any good sausage—I snuck into my parents' room. I was still a little scared, but my curiosity won out and no one offered me the poisoned apple when I pulled open the door. They were all there—mine, my brothers', my cousin Hélène's, my cousin Claude's, piled helter-skelter and *not yet wrapped!* I knew that the skates were for Bernard who'd been whining for them all year, that the records would be played till we were sick of them on the record-player Jacques had just bought for the 45 rpms with the central post that made my Grandmother Tremblay blush, that the cosmetics were for Hélène, the box of chocolates for her brother, Claude, who at twelve couldn't stand toys and whose only pleasure seemed to be stuffing his face.

All the others were doodads of no interest—silly things to fill a spoiled child's Christmas stocking—and a *book*. A real book, like the ones everyone else in the family read, with not many illustrations and *lots* of text. A pink cover with an illustration dominated by blue, yellow and red that depicted a little fair-haired boy asleep under a tree, another little boy, slightly older–his brother most likely—who was about to cover him with his jacket, a strangely dressed gentleman bending over them—a Zouave, in fact—and a Saint Bernard with a lolling tongue and a benevolent look. *L'Auberge de l'Ange-Gardien*. Comtesse de Ségur. Comtesse? What a funny name!

I was so excited I nearly sneezed. I stuck my head inside the presents and pinched my nose ... Nothing happened. The danger had passed. I could open the book.

But was I allowed to? Of course not. Christmas was still a few weeks away and it was absolutely forbidden to touch a present before December 25, on pain of sin! Venial maybe, but still a sin. *That* I'd have to confess! I could see myself kneeling in the dark, telling the priest that I'd read my Christmas present three weeks ahead of time ...

"And what did you do when your mother gave you your present on Christmas morning?"

"Umm, I pretended I was surprised."

"Another lie! You'll pay for this, young man!"

What a dilemma! I was holding what I wanted most in the world and I wasn't allowed to touch it!

It was, I think, one of the greatest temptations of my life. And I trembled as I succumbed to it, convinced that I was doing something very wrong—deceiving my parents, deserving a huge punishment such as having to fetch the coal from the shed behind the house to feed the furnace for the rest of the winter ... But I couldn't help myself, I wanted to know who those children were, and that man. And most of all, I who wasn't allowed to bring animals into the house, wanted to know who that dog belonged to! I opened the book, it cracked a little, I jumped and closed it again, and ran my hand over the shiny cover. I mustn't leave any evidence that I'd found it! The second time I dared to turn to the first page.

At first, everything was fine. "It was cold and dark; there was a steady drizzle; two children were asleep at the side of the main road, under a bushy old oak tree ... " though I thought that the first sentence, which covered *thirteen* lines, was very long. And the use of the semi-colon and the colon was still vague in my mind. But I understood, it described the illustration on the cover and I could refer to it whenever I wanted. I just had to apply the cover picture to the words and it was all more or less clear.

The first problem came two pages later, making me stare at the book, puzzled. On page nine, after a few brief dialogues in quotation marks that I understood easily, the Comtesse de Ségur wrote this:

"THE CHILD.—I don't care; I'm tall and strong; but he is a little boy; he cries when he's cold or when he's hungry."

"THE MAN.—Why are the two of you here?"

What were the words "man" and "child" doing there, followed by a period and a little line? Did it mean they were talking? Were you supposed to say the names of the characters out loud in your head before you read the rest? If so, it bothered me because I didn't want to hear myself say, "The child," before I read what the child had to say! That was really dumb! I didn't need it to help me understand, I wasn't stupid, so what was it doing there? Was there some reason that I didn't understand? I, a future playwright, was so repelled by that way of transcribing dialogue that after I'd started the ninth page ten or twelve times without finding an answer to my question, I started crying into my book. If I couldn't understand after three pages, what would it be like over a hundred and ninety? This terrible sorrow of a child who knows why he's crying and has no one to solve his problem, broke my heart. I was close to thinking that I was already being punished for my bad deed. I closed the book, telling myself that on Christmas morning someone in the family would explain it all and I'd finally be able to read *L'Auberge de l'Ange-Gardien*. It only half-relieved me though because, already too proud, I would have preferred to figure it out on my own. I blew my nose on the sleeve of my sweater as best I could and put the book back where I'd found it.

At the risk of being caught, I went to the closet nearly every day to open the book and try to figure out why Comtesse—it sounded like the name of a dog!—de Ségur had written her dialogues that way. Leafing through the book, I realized that there were dialogues like that right through the book and I slammed it shut, thinking that I'd never get to the end of the story because it upset me so much to see the characters' names in capitals all the time ... I was fixated on those dialogues and I started to hate the book before I'd got past page nine.

Christmas was coming and one day I saw my book wrapped in a big picture of a laughing Santa Claus.

And then one night I was struck by a question that had me rooted to the spot, unable to move, my heart in a vise: were all books written like that? And did it mean that I would never like to read?

***

My father wasn't allowed to bring alcohol into the house—since his marriage to Mama twenty years earlier, it was an unwavering rule that he'd never broken—except at Christmas, because, after all, he had to offer visitors something. And he'd take advantage of the season to seriously tie one on at the least opportunity. During the year, he drank beer with his friends at the tavern near home, but a week or two before Christmas I saw the discreet arrival of cases of beer and cartons of hard liquor (Bol's Geneva gin, rye, which Papa particularly liked, poor quality Scotch, a gallon of Quebec-made white wine—the revolting Québérac that my mother would serve in coloured glasses to the ladies, diluting it half-and-half with water and telling them: "Careful now, this is strong!"—green bottles, brown bottles, thin ones without shoulders and fat ones with square shoulders) that my Aunt Robertine and Mama carefully stowed under the kitchen sink where they were positive the men would never look. My Uncle Gérard and my Uncle Fernand, my father's brothers who lived with us, were also inclined to drink, to use a euphemism, and they absolutely must not know what we had in the house.

Starting at the beginning of December, my father would often ask, before he left for work around four p.m:

"Did you buy the liquor for the holidays, Nana?"

Mama replied: "I'm not crazy, I want some left for Christmas!"

Then he'd give her a pat on her plump rear-end.

"You know me too well."

And she'd give him a little smile.

"I sure do, and if I'd known I'd've made you without an elbow to bend!"

Over the Christmas holiday, Papa would start knocking back his little shots of rye around three p.m., was beet-red at four, wiping his face by five, and in a very good mood by suppertime. Whether or not there were visiting relatives he would propose toast after toast, tell stories that were more or less dirty, sing, loud and off-key, songs whose words he'd never really understood because he was deaf. When he really overdid it, Mama would position herself behind his chair and put her hand on his back; he'd apologize and stop for a few minutes, then he'd start up again even louder with a new one.

He was the life of the party at all the family get-togethers, making the men laugh and the women blush, and terrifying the children because he talked so loud, but he always knew when to stop and I never saw him so drunk as to disgrace us. In the middle of a toast, a song or a story, he'd say: "I may be deaf but I just heard my little warning bell. Time to stop!" Then he'd put down his glass, which usually meant, "The party's over!" because he'd then launch into a loud and malicious version of "O Canada" that everyone repeated in chorus, standing at attention with one hand over their hearts.

And the next morning, he would treat his hangover by starting his day with a beer cut with tomato juice. All my memories of Christmas morning feature the sight of my father, suffering from a terrible headache, trying to get his insides back in place with what he called "a little red beer."

On the Christmas morning in question, after pretending to be thrilled over presents I already knew about—all children think they're great actors—I excitedly tore the paper off my book by Comtesse de Ségur, and started reading L'Auberge de l'Ange-Gardien right away while my teary-eyed parents looked on. My mother ran her hand through my hair, which was cut too short for my liking, especially in winter.

"I told you, Armand, I knew he'd love to get a nice book for Christmas!"

My father was leaning over my shoulder and I could smell his beery breath that still contained the stench of last night's rye. He took the book from my hands.

"The Comtesse de Ségur ... Hey, is that a girl's book?"

"Oh, for heaven's sake! Look at the cover! There's three characters and they're all men!"

"If you say so ... But that one there, in the back, would you mind telling me what he's dressed up as?"

"He's a Zouave, Armand, I can't believe you've never seen a Zouave before."

"Oh, yeah, now that you mention it ... But it's the first one I've ever seen in colour ... I didn't think they had all those colours in their costumes, I thought they were ... I don't know ... grey, khaki maybe ... seems to me you don't go off to fight a war in red-and-blue puffy pants like that and a hat with a pompom on top."

To create a diversion, because my parents' arguments could last for hours, the bad faith of one pushing the other's to new limits, I asked one of the questions I'd been fretting about:

"How come her name's Comtesse?"

My mother frowned.

"What?"

"The woman that wrote the book, why's her name Comtesse?"

When I saw the little smile blossoming on her lips I knew right away that I'd slipped up and that I'd be hearing my mother describing my latest howler on the phone.

"Comtesse isn't her name ... ."

"So what is it, if isn't her name?"

"It's a title."

"Isn't the title *L'Auberge de l'Ange-Gardien*?"

"I mean it's a title of nobility ... A countess is, well, she's like a queen but not as important. It's like underneath a queen ... "

"She lives underneath a queen?"

"Michel, please, don't pretend you don't understand just to make me talk ... "

"I'm not pretending ... "

"I didn't say she *lives* underneath ... . How could I tell you that? When kings and queens have children they're called princes and princesses, you understand that, don't you?"

"Sure."

"So counts and countesses ... "

"They're the children of princes and princesses?"

"Michel, it's Christmas morning, but if you don't let me talk I'm going to box your ears! It's like ... I don't know, boy cousins and girl cousins, let's say ... Yes, that's it ... So the Comtesse de Ségur, she's probably got a boy cousin or a girl cousin that's a king or a queen somewhere in Russia ... "

"Have they got kings and queens in Russia?"

"No ... They used to have but not any more since the Communists took over ... Anyway, they weren't called kings and queens, they were called czars and ... What's the word, Armand, what's the feminine of czar?"

My father had long since gone back to his red beer.

"What're you talking about?"

My mother enunciates each word carefully so he'll understand.

"WHAT IS THE FEMININE OF CZAR?"

"The feminine of what?"

"CZAR! CZAR! THE CZAR OF RUSSIA!"

"I don't know ... Couldn't tell you ... Maybe czarette?"

My Grandmother Tremblay's voice comes to us from the other end of the apartment.

"It's czarina, the feminine of czar, and quit yelling like that on Christmas morning!"

My mother turns her head slightly.

"Thanks, Madame Tremblay. But we aren't yelling, we're having a discussion!"

My father wasn't really following what was going on.

"Who's that you're talking to?"

"YOUR MOTHER! SHE SAYS THE FEMININE OF CZAR IS CZARINA!"

"Czarina? Sounds like the name of some kind of fruit! Hey, Michel, want to eat a little czarina?"

He laughs, finishes his beer. My mother raises her forefinger.

"No more drinking till tonight, Armand! If you're that comical at nine a.m., what will you be like when the company gets here?"

He shrugged, but my mother knew he was going to obey.

I'd dived back into my reading, pretended to, rather, so I'd finally get to that bewildering page nine.

"Mama ... "

"Now what?"

"I've got another question."

"If you keep asking questions after every line you'll make me wish I hadn't bought you a book."

I had a very serious fit that lasted a long time when my mother confirmed what I'd already guessed: the characters' names were written out to show who was talking. As simple as that. And I didn't like it. As simple as that.

"I don't want to read any more! Ever!"

"What do you mean, you spoiled little brat! Don't want to read any more! You've just got to page nine in your very first book! Read a little more for pete's sake, you'll get used to it! Jeepers creepers, you aren't going to tell the Comtesse de Ségur how to write a book!"

She brought one hand to her mouth, the other to her heart.

"Now I've done it, I said a bad word on Christmas morning!"

"The other day Gramma Tremblay said that jeepers creepers isn't a bad word."

"And you, buster, aren't going to decide what's a bad word and what isn't. And never mind about Gramma Tremblay. Sometimes Gramma Tremblay's a little too broad-minded ... "

My grandmother's voice came to us again from the back of the apartment.

"I heard that, Nana ... "

"You aren't like your son—you've got ears like a gramophone horn!"

My grandmother laughed; there wouldn't be a spat. Anyway, the two women adored one another and their rows, always over ridiculous things, never lasted long.

All at once my mother softened, as she often did, letting out one of those long sighs of which you never knew if it signified exasperation or relief. She got up, checked that her new dress—a vast garment that looked vaguely impression-ist because of the blurred shapes in the design and the pastel colours, that she'd bought for next to nothing, as she said, at Dupuis Frères—wasn't stuck between her thighs, something she lived in dread of.

"Try another ten pages and if you still don't like it we'll buy you another one where the dialogues aren't written like that ... I don't think seventy-five cents is going to break us!"

"It isn't always like that? Other books aren't like that?"

Suddenly, for a long moment, my whole future hung on Mama's lips; it seemed to me that she had the power to decide if I would become a reader, like my grandmother, or someone who hated books, like my brother Bernard. I'd had enough time to bend my head over my book while waiting for her answer. I begged her inwardly, the way I'd been told to pray to the good Lord: "Say it isn't like that, Mama, say it's never like that in other books and I'm saved!"

"I haven't read every book that's been written since the beginning of Creation like your Grandma Tremblay has, but

I can tell you it's the first one I've ever seen written like that!"

I'd heard my grandmother coming closer while Mama was talking (a heavy step, a leg gliding along the floor) and she got to the dining room just in time to ask her daughter-in-law:

"You never read the Comtesse de Ségur when you were a child, Rhéauna? All her books are written like that."

My mother's dark eyes narrowed the way they did when she was about to let fly one of those retorts that were the joy of the whole family.

"The Comtesse de Ségur never made it to Saskatchewan, Madame Tremblay. Her boat ticket was only good to Montreal!"

Immediately I saw a beautiful princess standing on the deck of a ship docked in the port of Montreal with a case full of *L'Auberge de l'Ange-Gardien* sitting beside her. Something was wrong with that picture but I didn't have time to figure out what it was.

The two women were smiling; my mother turned towards the kitchen.

"Meanwhile, let me get busy with my turkey stuffing. I'd better start now if I want to feed our company tonight."

My grandmother settled into her rocking chair in front of the radio, but she didn't turn it on. She placed her hands flat on her knees. I liked to look at her beautiful hands with the bulging veins, worn down by decades of harsh work and cold-water laundry. My father used to say that you had to leave his mother alone when she was reading, that it was the great reward of her life, that she'd earned a peaceful old age.

"D'you want me to help you?"

"When I want to read with you in your bedroom you always say two people can't read together ... "

"Just let me give you a little advice, dear, then I'll leave you in peace ... When you get to the names of characters, pass over them as if they weren't there, don't read them in your head, and everything will be fine."

"You don't have to read everything in a book?"

"You read what you want to read, sweetheart."

***

I couldn't really disregard the characters' names while I was reading, but I was soon caught up in the story. The little children lost by the roadside, the brave Zouave who took them under his protective wing, the beautiful innkeeper who took them all in, feeding and lodging them and only asking them to transport the milk ... *Transport the milk?* As a city child who only had to open the apartment door every morning to see quarts of milk waiting on the doormat, I found it hard to imagine that you could get your milk directly from a cow or your eggs from under a hen ... I learned all kinds of things about life in the country, the names of trees and flowers, dishes I'd never heard of; after fifteen pages I was madly in love with the dog, Captain, and I was dreaming of having an innkeeper for a mother ...

Eventually, though, the two little boys, Jacques and Paul, seemed really weird. They talked incredibly well for farmers' sons, pronouncing every syllable, never omitting the "ne" from a negative, they were polite and perfect and they got on my nerves. Because I couldn't identify with them, I suppose. They were children, but children like I'd never seen in my life. If anyone in my class had talked like that, he'd get a faceful of fist, fast! Besides that, they seemed to absolutely want people to feel sorry for them and I hated that: okay, so their mother was dead; their father had disappeared, kidnapped by soldiers, okay; if they'd told us they were sick and crippled, I wouldn't have been surprised! A tiny worm of jealousy was starting to curl up inside my belly *because they were in a book* and I tried to go a little faster on the pages where they appeared. I preferred the secondary characters who, I thought were funny: the Zouave in his ridiculous get-up who talked about the war as if it were a bingo game; the innkeeper and her sister, the beautiful Elfy, whom I'd have liked to have as cousins and drink fresh milk and eat raw eggs with; the priest, who was surprisingly nice and not a snob like ours; most of all, General Durakin, who threw money out the windows, laughing and drinking champagne ... It was the first really long story that I'd read; I was thrilled to be able to follow everything easily and hypnotized by the number of pages the author had been able to write!

And then, in the middle of the description of a meal I came upon something that left me perplexed, to say the least: "Next came a *haricot* of lamb with potatoes." I re-read the sentence very carefully. No, I hadn't made a mistake ...

"Gramma ... "

"Yes, dear."

"Look at this, here, read ... "

"Is there something you don't understand?"

She read the whole sentence several times, frowning.

"Rhéauna ... "

"What is it, Madame Tremblay?"

"Can you come here a minute?"

My mother arrived, drying her hands.

"I'm afraid I won't have enough bread for my stuffing ... "

"Read this, will you ... "

"Hold the book, my hands are dirty."

She read the sentence too, bending over the book.

Then all three of us looked at it.

"Mama, *haricots* are beans like in pork and beans, aren't they?"

"Yes ... But in France it can mean other kinds of beans too, I think."

My grandmother went back to the book.

"How can a lamb have beans, will you tell me that? Beans are a vegetable, they don't grow inside a sheep! Is she crazy or what? That countess never cooked a lamb in her life!"

"Maybe the printer made a mistake."

"But it doesn't say: 'Next came a lamb with beans and potatoes, 'it says: next came a *haricot* of lamb with potatoes!'"

"Maybe there's a part of the lamb that the French call a *haricot* ... "

"That's possible, you know."

"But what part would it be?"

"The kidneys. That's right, kidneys are shaped a little like beans."

"Hey, that's right, and in English they say *kidney beans.*"

"That must be it then."

"All right, Michel, I think we've figured it out ... I don't know what else it could be ... It's lamb kidneys and spuds."

"And beans ... "

"No, no, Madame Tremblay, it would say: 'then came a *haricot* of lamb with beans and potatoes.' That's not what it says."

"Can you eat that, lamb kidneys?"

"I guess so ... After all, you can eat veal kidneys and pork kidneys."

"If you say so. So you mean it's just lamb kidneys and spuds?"

"Looks like it."

"No vegetables along with?"

"Doesn't sound like it."

"Not even some peas?"

"Guess not."

"They're strange, the French! And it's supposed to be them that invented cooking! Honestly! I'd be ashamed to put out a plate with just meat and potatoes on it ... Any self-respecting woman's going to serve at least one vegetable!"

"Maybe they can't afford it ... "

"Come on, Rhéauna, they're farmers! They must have vegetables coming out their ears! Anyway, they can keep their *haricot* of lamb and potatoes, I wouldn't eat it for all the gold in the world!"

"Bet it's good though ... "

"Rhéauna, you'd eat anything!"

"If you say so ... "

And that was why, all through my childhood, I thought that when the French wanted to say "kidneys" they said "beans."

***

It took me a few days to read *L'Auberge de l'Ange-Gardien*. I spent a good part of the week between Christmas and New Year's curled up in one corner of the big living room sofa, my head in the France of the Second Empire, surprised by words like *fricot* or *pies-grièches*, thrilled all the same that the children, whom I finally learned to tolerate, got back their father, disappointed that Captain, the dog, didn't play a bigger part in the story ... I stumbled seriously over the account of the siege of Sebastopol and finally gave up on it because I couldn't understand a thing and besides, I wasn't interested in battles.

With the father back, the two couples married, General Durakin happy, the two children settled down, loved, pampered, spoiled, stuffed with *haricot* of lamb and potatoes, I closed the book, drunk on images, sounds, smells. And so proud that I'd been able to finish a whole book that was *a hundred and ninety pages long!* I hadn't understood it all, far from it, but I'd grasped most of the story and I couldn't wait to go back to school in January and boast about my accomplishment.

My mother, my Aunt Robertine, and my Grandmother Tremblay were eating the remains of a pie in the dining room.

I slammed *L'Auberge de l'Ange-Gardien* down on the table, making as much noise as I could to get their attention.

"I want another one!"

TINTIN AU CONGO

Hergé

For a long time I resisted Tintin. After all, I hadn't graduated from baby books just to go back to picture books with bright colours and illustrations that were more important than the words! I tended to look down on the little boys sitting at the round tables in the children's room at the Municipal Library with their noses in *Tintin in America* or *The Seven Crystal Balls*, while I plunked down my second volume of *The Mysterious Island* or the latest Biggles, which I'd devoured one Saturday afternoon while listening—already—to the Metropolitan Opera. Heads would turn in my direction and I'd look away, saying a little too loudly to the librarian, who was rather amused by my pretentiousness: "I hope you've still got some I haven't read yet." The other children must have hated me. Quite rightly too because I'm sure I was really loathsome.

***

When I turned eight, on June 25, 1950, my cousin Hélène gave me a shiny quarter and said: "Go and join the Municipal Library, I think it costs thirty cents." (Why have Quebeckers always called a quarter *thirty cents*? Maybe simply because of a lack of logic, but who knows?)

So off I went with my nose in the air and my quarter hidden inside a knot I'd made with one corner of my handkerchief. It was one of my mother's tricks that she was very proud of but that, in practice, wasn't very convenient: when it was time to pay on the streetcar or at the movies, I always kept the other people waiting.

That day though, I was rich—at the time, twenty-five cents represented five ice cream cones or five bags of Maple Leaf chips, two-and-a-half orders of fries, nearly four Coffee Crisps, it was my birthday, a beautiful day, I had the whole summer ahead of me to binge on reading. I'd often gone to exchange books for my Grandmother Tremblay, along with my cousin Hélène, or Jeannine, my Aunt Marguerite's daughter, and I'd ask them: "Do you have to be as old as Gramma to come and get books here?" This time it was my turn: I was going for myself, and I'd be able to choose all the books I wanted!

The Municipal Library was a good distance from home: to get there, I had to walk down Fabre Street from Gilford to Rachel, then negotiate the entire length of Parc Lafontaine, from north to south. And cross Sherbrooke Street!

My mother, panicky because I'd be doing so by myself for the first time, had warned me: "If you come home dead and run over by a car or crippled for life, I'll never speak to you again!"

I knew Parc Lafontaine inside out because I'd spent days there, when I was a small child, with my brothers, Jacques and Bernard, and my cousins, Hélène, Jeannine, and Lise, all of them older than me, who had brought me there on hot summer days when my mother had trouble getting around because of her weight. Each of them in turn had sacrificed a day of holidays to give her a break from me: Jacques read me my first Babar; Bernard showed me how to climb the wooden ladders; Hélène played at being the actress who's looking after a poor little boy (she hid me behind a tree, "discovered" me, threw herself at me thinking I was such a pitiful sight, kissed me, adopted me ... and then started over twenty-five times to hone her performance, all in English, needless to say, because she wanted a career in Hollywood); Lise made me punch holes in the sky with my feet, pushing me too hard on the baby swings; and Jeannine told me stories that thrilled me. I'd been happy there and now I was wild at the thought of what was waiting for me across the street: I practically ran down the shady lanes and across the cement bridge between the two lakes, my hand firmly gripping the handkerchief deep in my pocket, heart pounding and short of breath.

When I got to Sherbrooke Street—crowded, noisy, scary after the calm of the park—I did as my mother said: "Take a good long look to your left, then a good long look to your right, and when you don't see any cars coming *in both directions* for at least two blocks, then you can run across. And not before! If you don't do as I say your nose will grow like Pinocchio's and Mama will know!" I didn't take any chances; it's true that Mama always ended up knowing everything and I didn't want to end the day with a four-foot-long nose decorated with a nest of squawking birds!

I hesitated before going into the children's room; the door to it was located on Montcalm Street, on the Sherbrooke hill, and underneath the adults' which at that point was the only one I'd visited. I looked in the window. Nearly empty. There were three huge round, solid walnut tables with short legs—I went back there last year, during the scandal over the floors that were in danger of collapsing under the weight of the books, and I saw the same tables, forty-two years later, with the same smell of varnish but darkened by wear and time, and I nearly burst into tears—and I saw a little girl with braids, I remember very clearly, bent over a huge picture book; two little boys who seemed bored to death and for whom the library was probably a punishment;

the librarian herself, stiff and bespectacled, with nothing to do because it was too nice a day for children to think about improving themselves.

I was so shy, I'd never be able to talk to that stern-looking woman! Finally though I continued down Montcalm Street to the wide-open door and went inside, enjoying the coolness and silence after the sweltering heat and the rumbling noise of Sherbrooke Street. Seeing my awkwardness and guessing, probably, that I was a new convert, the woman smiled. Her face was completely transformed; suddenly it wasn't stern at all, but engaging and warm. There was even a little flicker of teasing in her eyes before this poor, petrified child, a little like when my cousin Jeannine finished one of her fantastic tales that terrified me so. She had a winning smile, but a mischievous sparkle in her eyes.

I approached the solid counter behind which she was standing and as I was making my way towards her, I could make out the smell of the books, a mixture of dust and printer's ink, the same delicious smell that came from the ones my Grandmother Tremblay borrowed. I looked farther away, to the lady's left. Tons of books, blue, red, brown, grey, neatly arranged on miles of shelves! Upstairs, in the adults' room, you never saw the books, you had to fill out little forms and hand them to the librarians who then disappeared onto hidden staircases, but here ... four huge walls of books surrounded me, crushed me! A whole lifetime of reading!

"You want to join?"

I couldn't speak so I nodded as I took out my handkerchief and started to undo the knot. I held up my quarter, then carefully set it down on the varnished table.

"You can put that back in your pocket, it doesn't cost anything."

All that didn't cost anything? Really and truly?

"Put it back in your pocket, Michel, before you forget it."

Michel? She knew my name?

"How come you know my name?"

She turned pink, just barely.

"Your mother called to see if you'd got here. Your name is Michel Tremblay, isn't it?"

I was so ashamed I'd have disappeared into the floor if I could.

But I only pouted as I hung my head.

"I'm not a baby, why did she phone?"

"She doesn't think you're a baby, she just wanted to be sure you got here all right ... You're a long way from home, you know ... "

She took out a long form and handed it to me with a smile.

"Can you fill that out by yourself?"

"I just told you, I'm not a baby!"

***

"Did you think I couldn't get there on my own?"

"No."

"So why did you phone?"

"It was the first time you'd gone so far by yourself."

"So that's it, you thought I couldn't ... "

"No, no! Let me speak!"

"So why did you call?"

"Michel! I'm your mother! I've got the right to do what I want in my own house! If I want to call up Soucisse when I send you out for milk, or the presbytery when you go to confession, I'll do it! I ask you, does it make any sense for you to lecture me! Find me one mother, buster, who'll look up the library's phone number because she's worried about her child who's walking halfway across the island of Montreal for the first time! Would you be happier if I didn't look after you, if I acted as if I couldn't care less if I ever saw you again?"

"I was only going to the library, Mama, not to the other end of the earth!"

"At your age, that's pretty darn close to the other end of the earth! And I didn't want that woman lending you just any old book either. After all, we don't know her! What did she give you, here, let's see ... "

"She didn't lend me any thing, I picked them out myself!"

"She didn't even give you any advice?"

"Course not, she let me go around and look at the rows of books ... All she said was I can take six books for two weeks instead of just three because it's summer holidays ... "

"She didn't follow you or anything?"

"Course not ... "

"But what if you'd picked out books that're too old for you?"

"It's the children's room, Mama ... "

"Children aren't all the same age, buster! Now show me those books ... I'm going to call up that woman again, that's no way to behave! Does she get paid for just stamping the books? We trust them with our children and they don't even look after them ... The Comtesse de Ségur! Again! You could recite her by heart, your Comtesse de Ségur, try something new! What else have you got there? Don't hide the other books ... Six of them! You'll wear out your eyes! And what about your twenty-five cents, what did you do with that?"

"What twenty-five cents?"

"Michel, don't make me waste my time. Hélène gave you twenty-five cents ... "

"That was for my birthday! It's a present! I can do whatever I want with my twenty-five cents!"

"That was to pay for joining the library and it's free to join the library!"

"Did you ask her that too?"

"Yes, of course I did! And I also asked her to call me back if you weren't polite with her! Michel! Michel, come back here! I hate it when he goes away and I haven't finished talking to him! Michel! I don't care if it's your birthday, you come right back here or you'll have me to answer to!"

***

So, to get back to Tintin.

It's my birthday, one year later to the day, so I'm nine years old.

Mama, my Aunt Robertine, and even my Grandmother Tremblay have been banging around in the kitchen since morning to get ready for my birthday party. It already smells of pound cake and gingersnaps. On one corner of the table my grandmother is mixing her famous molasses cookie dough so she can make me her Charlevoix bears' paws that I'm so crazy about. I decide that I'll try not to eat too much, so I won't get sick to my stomach like I do at Christmas ... and Easter ... When the three women in the household are all cooking at the same time, the whole family goes out of control and stomach aches aren't rare. If I really overdo it, my grandmother tells my mother: "Rhéauna, the cows are in the corn!" and my plate disappears as if by magic, even if I kick up a fuss.

It's one o'clock and my little friends won't be here till three. I'm nervous, I prowl the house restlessly, I get kicked out of the kitchen every five minutes because I always have my finger in the pie dough or the cake batter, I try to read while I rock in my mother's big chair on the balcony. Nothing interests me, not the Comtesse de Ségur, not Jules Verne, my new passion, whom I've just discovered with *Five Weeks in A Balloon*. Two hours is a long time to wait, way too long!

I go down the stairs, take up my post in the middle of the sidewalk, and look towards Mont-Royal Street to see if my friends are coming home with my presents ... I saw Madame Rouleau, Madame Jodoin, and Madame Guérin go out with their children a few minutes earlier and I imagine them choosing fantastic presents for me at Messier's or Woolworth's. Well, maybe not fantastic, they aren't rich, but nice presents anyway, that I'll be so excited to open.

"Will you quit standing and watching like that, those friends of yours won't be coming for two hours—*if* they come!"

She wipes her floury hands on her apron, then sits in her rocking chair to sip a Coke.

"That's not who I was watching for, Mama!"

"Who was it then? Santa Claus? Honestly, Michel, how stupid do you think I am?"

Aunt Robertine comes out next, patting her forehead and cheeks. Then she wipes her armpits with her apron and my mother rolls her eyes.

"For the love of God, Bartine, do that inside!"

My aunt doesn't seem to have heard her.

"It's as hot as the dickens in there! Besides, who ever heard of baking cakes in the middle of June!"

Mama turns towards her.

"If his birthday was in January we wouldn't be able to come out and cool off while they're baking! We'd come down with a double pneumonia, so don't complain!"

I'm sitting on the bottom step of the stairs to the balcony, watching ants carrying away some dandelion remains.

"Mamaaaa ... "

My mother leans over the railing, her elbows resting on it.

"When he whines like that, he wants something ... Now what?"

"Know what you could do to help me wait?"

"Listen to this, Bartine, I think we're going to have a good laugh. How could we help you wait, Michel? Bring you the Barnum and Bailey circus? Barbara Ann Scott and the Hollywood Ice Revue? Laurel and Hardy? Abbott and Costello?"

"Noooo ... "

"That's good ... "

I stood up, climbed a few steps, gave her my most winning smile and my most adoring look.

My mother shakes her head a little.

"What is it now?"

"Well ... I've got five presents, right?"

"How should I know, I haven't counted them ... "

"I did though ... Listen ... to help me wait ... "

"Stop right there! I see exactly where you're going! And the answer is, absolutely not!"

"Just one, Mama!"

"I said absolutely not! I know we've spoiled you rotten, but there's a limit!"

"Just one! A little one! The very littlest one! One that isn't even important!"

"Michel, your party is this afternoon when your friends are here and you'll open your presents then and not before, and that's that. Understand?"

My eyes are already full of tears, my lower lip is quivering.

"And don't make a scene on your birthday!"

My Aunt Robertine has set her Coke down next to her chair.

"You know how stubborn he is, Nana ... "

"Don't you start! I know what's on your mind too!"

"He's going to carry on all afternoon and he'll be worn out by the time his friends get here ... "

"Bartine, we aren't going to let that child make the rules! He's a big enough pest as it is!"

At that point my grandmother puts in an appearance and my hope of opening a present right away goes up a notch.

"What's going on? I can hear you yelling in the toilet all the way at the other end of the house!"

"Michel wants to open his presents ... "

"I said one present!"

"And don't interrupt! I say no, but Bartine's taking his side ... "

"I'm not on his side, but if it'll give us some peace ... "

"Will you give him the moon if he asks for it, just to get some peace?"

"He wouldn't ask for that ... "

"I'm not so sure!"

Now the three of them are leaning against the wood and wrought-iron railing. It's an image that will be engraved in me forever: three silhouettes spattered with flour, looking at me with different expressions: despondency on my mother, who suspects she won't win because she loves me too much and can't refuse me anything; something like greed on my Aunt Robertine, who's at least as impatient as I am to see me unwrap her present; compassion on my Grandmother Tremblay, who always understands everything.

Aunt Robertine gives Mama a surreptitious look.

"We could let him open my present, Nana, I wouldn't mind ... And it would keep him busy for part of the afternoon, *if you know what I mean* (this last in English, as was my mother's reply).

"*I know exactly what you mean and I still think it's not a good idea ... *"

I give them my devastating little smile, the one my mother can never resist.

"We've started taking English at school you know, so soon I'll understand everything ... "

The three women try not to laugh; I've won.

I let out a whoop of joy as I climb the stairs.

Mama turns to her sister-in-law.

"If only you were like that with your own kids, Bartine!"

***

It's rectangular, flat, hard: a game! It's true, it will keep me busy while I wait for my friends to arrive. I start to tear the wrapping paper.

"Read the card first, Michel!"

(She wants to show that she still has at least a little authority over me.)

Okay, okay: "Happy birthday, blablabla ... your loving godmother ... " Wet kiss, thank you, thank you, you're so nice ...

Wait, it isn't a game, it's too thin ... Seems more like a picture book ... Oh, no!

Tintin au Congo.

There's a moment's wavering in the dining room where the scene takes place. After all, I can't throw the book at them, and stomp off to my room and slam the door, *it's a birthday present and I asked to open it before the others!* And my godmother couldn't know that I'm not interested in Tintin.

My mother, somewhat worried at my lack of enthusiasm, asks me:

"Are you glad?"

The actor regains the upper hand and I manage a look that could be interpreted as "surprised and happy."

"Oh yes! Sure! Wow! And I've never read any Tintin!"

"Really? And there I was scared that you already knew this one by heart! You can read it right away, you know ... Go sit on the balcony, I'll bring you a nice cold Coke ... "

"No, Bartine, no Coke before his party ... "

Mama suspects something, I'm sure of it. She looks at me as if she could read the disappointment on my face despite the act I'm putting on. After all, she can't say, "I told you it wasn't a good idea!" or something of the sort. Manufacturing a big forced grin that, I think, takes them in, I hug my book to my heart and head for the balcony.

Aunt Robertine is pink with delight.

"It'll keep him quiet till the birthday party ... "

Mama heads for the kitchen, fixing a loose strand of hair with a bobby pin.

"Sure it will! Go ahead and dream!"

***

To my amazement, *Tintin in the Congo* makes me laugh out loud. It was the racist version that's nowhere to be found anymore, that some people claim never even existed, but at the age of nine I don't know what racism is and I have a good laugh when Tintin gives a bar of soap to the black people who discover when they wash that they're actually pale black like Tintin's allies, they're all brothers and there must be peace between them ... It's a little like a rehearsal for the story about the wicked Iroquois and the good Hurons and I think it's funny. The dialogues written in a sort of pidgin language have me rolling on the floor: "Him good boy, Mistah White," the Leopard Man terrifies me, going down the river in a canoe excites me, the White Father, who resembles our own Père Ambroise, is jolly and amusing and he moves me with his devotion ... Today, that book would make me shudder, but the little boy who reads the adventures of Tintin and Milou, the talking dog, on the balcony of the Fabre Street apartment, knows nothing about either Belgium or the Belgian Congo, he has no idea about colonialism even if, as a Québécois, he's been a cultural victim of it since birth, and he's devouring his first Tintin book with no ulterior motives, happy to discover that Tintin isn't all that boring after all. And forgets for a while that a birthday party is being organized for him in the kitchen and in the aisles of the stores on Mont-Royal Street.

**

"I finished!"

Three heads turn in my direction. The smell of cake batter and sweat fills the kitchen.

"What d'you mean, you finished?"

"Finished what?"

"My Tintin, what d'you think?"

My mother straightens up, pushing back an unruly lock of hair. Her forehead and her hair are covered with flour.

"Michel! You haven't had that book for half an hour!"

"I know, but it doesn't take long to read, it's mostly pictures and hardly any writing."

"Don't put your book on my pie crust! And I want you to go right back and read it the way it's supposed to be read! You probably don't even know what it's about, you went through it so fast! You little brat! And don't think we're going to let you open another present! Just because you got your way once, you aren't going to get it all day! You aren't going to make fun of us all day."

"I didn't want to open any other presents ... "

"Michel Tremblay! I know you so well there's times when I'd like to trade you in for another child, just to have some surprises!"

My grandmother has put her hand on my mother's.

"Don't yell at him so much, Nana, it's his birthday."

"Every day's his birthday if you ask me! No matter what I say to him, one of you always comes to his defence. He's a big spoiled brat because there's too many mothers around him!"

She takes my hand, leads me through the whole house, lifts me up by the armpits when we get to the balcony and plops me into the rocking chair.

"I don't want you getting out of that chair till you've read it! Not even to make peepee! Don't say you've read that book, Michel, it isn't true ... "

"Yes it is."

"And don't talk back unless you want me to put up a note to send your friends away because your birthday party's been called off!"

"I don't want a birthday party!"

"One more word out of you and you *won't* have one, understand? Do you understand?"

Between two sobs—I can't help crying and I'm humiliated—I open the book and hold it out to Mama.

"You can look if you want, I'm not a liar! Look, there's hardly anything to read!"

She takes the book, leafs through it at first abruptly, then lingers over a few pages.

"Would you look at that! He's right! There's nothing to read in this darn book! There's hardly anything but these big huge pictures. Here, this picture takes up a whole page! And it's full of naked niggers! What kind of book did she buy you anyway? God in Heaven, the woman's taken leave of her senses!"

She's already off, with the book under her arm.

"Bartine! Bartine! Where did you buy that book, will you tell me? It's full of people running around naked!"

My mother isn't usually the least bit scrupulous and I'm surprised at her reaction. I hear bits of an argument, Mama shouting, Aunt Robertine blowing her nose, my grandmother, as usual, being the conciliator.

I'm convinced that my birthday party is ruined and I cry even harder as I rock in the big wooden chair.

When I stop rubbing my eyes, my Grandmother Tremblay is beside me. Inside the house, peace has returned, or at any rate the shouting has stopped.

"Don't worry about it, sweetheart, they're all worked up because of the party, but everything's going to be fine ... When they yell like that it isn't because they're angry, it's because they're afraid that they won't finish on time, that the party won't be a success, that the cake will be flat as a pancake, that the cookies will burn ... You'll see, it will be a terrific party and everyone will have fun ... "

"I hate it when they yell like that ... "

"Of course you do, but you know very well that it's always like that ... and it never lasts very long."

"What about my Tintin?"

"Here it is. Did you really read the whole thing?"

"Sure ... "

"Will you read me some of it?"

A grandmother that's interested in Tintin? Wait till I tell my friends when they get here!

"Okay!"

"Let gramma have your place, dear. But you'll read, eh, it's not like when you were little. Now you're going to read and I'll listen!"

I make myself comfortable between her knees, because for a while now, I've been too heavy to sit on her lap, and open *Tintin au Congo*. There's a strong smell of Florida water and for a moment I feel dizzy.

Unless you've read to your grandmother on your ninth birthday, you don't know a thing about happiness!

LES ENFANTS DU CAPITAINE GRANT
(Captain Grant's Children)

Jules Verne

During my teenage years, whatever I knew about natural history, geography or physics came more from reading Jules Verne than from the boring lessons we were given in school. The teaching brothers were full of good will, some even tried to liven up their classes, but they couldn't compete with the prose of the favourite author of my twelve-year-old self—stories that practically launched us into the sky at the same time they were explaining how to do so, or that plunged us to the heart of the oceans while describing every fish we met.

I realized fairly early that I liked to learn from stories and novels rather than from physics or history textbooks; even now, I prefer historical novels to so-called "serious" biographies, and it seems to me that I learn more about Nero or Joan of Arc in a novel by Hubert Montheillet—who describes in minute detail what they wore, what they ate, and how they lived—than in any scholarly work that merely analyzes the facts instead of bringing the characters back to life. To understand the past I need human complexity and atmosphere. I need descriptions to be part of a story if I'm to grasp the laws of physics. Or the life of animals. And I can't deny that I prefer a nice fat lie made up by a good storyteller like Alexandre Dumas *père* to a boring account of the facts by a learned and overly objective historian. I couldn't care less whether Louis XIV had a twin or not, because I felt as if I really had lived in the court of the young Sun King when I read *Le Vicomte de Bragelonne*; it bugs me when someone says that the *Nautilus* would have been flattened like a pancake at thirty fathoms deep if it had been built exactly the way Jules Verne described it—apparently his calculations were flawed—because I felt as if I'd boarded it, as if I'd travelled deep in the sea over more than four hundred pages and for me, that's what matters!

I read *all* the descriptions, without skipping even one; I liked the simple and precise style—it's often said that he was a great popularizer—as much as the educational content: I learned about sea currents and life in the ocean depths in *Twenty Thousand Leagues Under the Sea*; about air currents in *Five Weeks in a Balloon*; the great steppes in *Michel Strogoff*; the Argentinean pampas and the Australian outback in *Captain Grant's Children*; the American Civil War in *North Against South*; the thickness of earth's crust and its composition in *Journey to the Centre of the Earth* ... I was dazzled by the construction of the enormous cannon that would propel onto the moon a cannonball inhabited by humans (*From Earth to the Moon*); intrigued by the invention of the ancestor of cinema (*The Castle of the Carpathians*); amazed to learn at the end of *The Southern Star* about the diamond that turned pink from its stay in the gizzard of an ostrich!

Jules Verne couldn't use a technical term or a foreign word without a lengthy explanation, and I'm grateful to him for that, because he taught me patience and curiosity. He even showed me how to use my dictionary intelligently when his explanations, detailed though they were, were insufficient. Thanks to him I discovered the pleasure of wandering through the dictionary for hours, even forgetting why I'd opened it in the first place ...

My teachers were often surprised at my general knowledge of physics, geography or natural history, but they understood when I waved a copy of *Robur the Conqueror* or *The Tribulations of a Chinese Gentleman*. Unfortunately, they held me up as an example, which didn't help my popularity at the Saint-Pierre-Clavet school.

***

The first fictional character with whom I identified completely, to the point of actually making myself sick, was Robert Grant, the young hero of *Captain Grant's Children*. It was one of the most important books of my late childhood, and I have a very clear memory of everything around my reading of it.

Robert Grant was twelve years old, like me, but his destiny was so much more fascinating that after a few pages, I didn't know if I liked him or loathed him, strictly out of jealousy.

His father, a Scottish master mariner, had been shipwrecked two years earlier—this was in 1864—somewhere on the 37th parallel; he'd been taken prisoner by some natives or other but had managed to send a message out to sea in a bottle. Lord Glenarvan, another Scottish sailor, had found the message, sopping-wet and therefore hard to read, in the belly of a whale; lucky Robert Grant had set out around the world to search for his father in a boat, the *Duncan*, accompanied by the lord and his young wife, Robert's sister, the lovely Mary, and a French geographer named Paganel, who had chosen the wrong boat. Now was that a life for a boy of twelve?

I had borrowed the three volumes of *Captain Grant's Children* from the Municipal Library and I slept with them, the one I was reading against my head so I could breathe it in even while I was asleep, the other two arranged on the blanket and subject to travel during the night according to how I moved in my sleep—a comforting presence between my legs, on my feet, or in the small of my back. I still sleep in the company of the books I'm reading: I rarely put them on my bedside table, but not one since *Captain Grant's Children* has so haunted my nights.

I read Robert Grant's adventures for as long as possible, until my mother threatened to remove the bulb from my bedside light, and then during part of the night I dreamed about crossing the Atlantic, the Magellan Straits, the landscapes of Chile, the Andes Cordillera ... My bed was a boat that readily left my bedroom on Cartier Street to speed towards the 37th parallel in search of the source of the Gulf Stream.

I was becoming an accomplished sailor along with Robert Grant; I was learning how to ride a magnificent black Argentinean horse in the company of Thalcave, the handsome, half-naked Patagonian whose picture on page 95 troubled me so much; I forded the Rio de Raque and the Rio de Tubal; I climbed the porphyry walls—the *quebradas*—I searched in vain for my father deep in the sequoia forests or on snow-covered mountain peaks. It was said of Robert Grant that he grew and developed quickly, that he was becoming a man; as for me, I read in the midst of cake or gingersnap crumbs and remained a desperately envious child who didn't have a grandiose destiny.

One episode in particular kept me awake all one night. I had a fever and couldn't go to school the next morning, to the great annoyance of my mother who suspected that *Captain Grant's Children* was behind all this unchannelled agitation. But the incident also marked the start of one of the most wonderful adventures of my life ...

Towards the middle of the first part of the novel, the men on the expedition decide to walk across first Chile and then Argentina in search of Captain Grant, while the women on board the *Duncan* go back through the Magellan Strait to wait for them on the Atlantic coast. I was sad to leave Mary Grant and Lady Glenarvan, but I was also very excited at the prospect of crossing South America on foot.

I was absolutely captivated by the mountain landscapes that Robert Grant and his friends encountered—I who knew only Mt. Royal, an insignificant hill, a place for Montrealers to go on Sunday walks, that I could glimpse from my balcony at the end of Mont-Royal Street. But the Andes Cordillera! The glaciers, the torrents hundreds of metres high (it said in my Larousse dictionary, printed in Canada, that a meter was equivalent to three feet, three inches), the rocky plateaus that hung suspended in mid air; the wind and rain storms that struck without warning and stopped so abruptly that you wondered if they'd actually happened; the pink sunrises; the orange sunsets! The food, which consisted of dried meat, grasses seasoned with hot peppers, freshly-killed game, water from mountain torrents and prairie streams, made my mouth water, offering a change from the eternal mashed potatoes and the inevitable number one canned peas! How could I ever eat shepherd's pie again?

Then I got to the chapter that practically made me levitate. At twelve thousand feet in the air, our friends had decided to spend the night on an icy plateau overhanging the vast valley they would start to cross in the days to come, to get to the Argentinean pampas. The night passes without incident, everyone's exhausted but happy, and they all sleep well. At dawn though a horrible crashing wakes them up and to quote Jules Verne:

> Owing to a phenomenon peculiar to the Cordillera's an entire massif several miles wide shifted and slipped towards the plain.
> "An earthquake!" exclaims Paganel.

The plateau where they'd taken refuge was tumbling down the mountain! I was there, falling with them, the snowy peaks were swirling around me, the mountains themselves were changing shape, the sky which was barely beginning to turn white was pitching as it had when I was crossing the Strait of Magellan on board the *Duncan*, my tent was wrapping itself around my legs, guns, firewood, kitchen utensils, *embers from the fire that hadn't been completely doused* went past me, touching me, I was riding a colossal roller coaster that was hurling me mercilessly towards the bottom of the valley, I was racing to my death, I was nearly dead already, nestled in my bed, my eyes wide open, my wildly beating heart exploding in my chest.

The worst thing was that at the beginning of the next chapter, with the earthquake subdued and the men slowly getting over their fright, *Robert Grant had disappeared!* Panic in Chile and in a ravaged bed on Cartier Street. The men looked in vain for the child over a period of three days while I, I'd stopped living: Robert Grant could not die, *I could not die*, the story couldn't move on without me, there were three hundred pages left, I was the hero, it was I who'd lost his father and had left Scotland to travel the world in search of him, it was I who was becoming a man in the midst of some Patagonians and master mariners, Jules Verne, my favourite author from any country and any time, didn't have the right to drop me like that!

Then came deliverance through one of the most powerful images from my childhood, one that forty years later I still summon if I happen to be suffering from insomnia, because I know it will help me get to sleep no matter what problem is keeping me awake: after three days of anxiety at the thought of never finding the lost child, Lord Glenarvan spots a speck in the sky, far, far away on the horizon ... the speck gets bigger ... and a huge Andean condor approaches, holding Robert Grant in his claws! The illustration showed the youth suspended by his clothes in the same pose as Christ in Michelangelo's *Pietà*. For three days I'd been transported by a condor! My emotion made me abruptly shut the book and cradle it. I tried to relive those three days, to see again, suspended in the air, the Andes Cordillera glide by under me, the nest hidden on a high granite peak, the hunger, the thirst—but exaltation too, at knowing you've been treated for three days like the son of the great condor!

They shot down the condor, Robert Grant regained consciousness, but I still hung suspended from the condor's claws by my torn clothes; I didn't want to come back down, I wanted to stay up there on the roof of the world—at least until the next day—and I switched off my bedside lamp, hoping that I'd dream about a powerful wind and vast silky wings.

My parents were very worried. I was running a fever but I had no other symptoms of the flu or even a cold. After a few days Mama tried to confiscate *Captain Grant's Children*, but whatever was wrong with me got worse and she gave me back the three yellowing, dusty volumes, sighing like a martyr.

Then a conversation we had when I started to feel better was going to change a lot of things.

It was noon, Mama had just brought me a big bowl of chicken soup, with some soda biscuits that I liked to soften in the broth before I ate them.

"I'm really glad you like to read, Michel, but if that's what is making you so sick I'm going to buy you a hockey stick so you'll build up some muscles!"

"If you only knew how wonderful it is, Mama!"

"So wonderful it's making you sick?"

"I'm not sick ... I'm dreaming."

"If your dreams give you a fever, Michel, they can't be all that wonderful."

"Read it yourself, you'll see!"

She had picked up the book and was leafing through it, sighing.

"I haven't got time. It's too big. And it's for children your age, not an old woman like me ... "

"You aren't that old ... "

"That's what you think ... I'm fifty-three!"

"True ... I guess you are."

"Careful you don't spill your soup now ... I just changed your bed and I don't feel like doing it again. Now tell me the story in that book so I'll have some kind of idea of what's going on in your little head ... "

It was not so much the story of *Captain Grant's Children* that disturbed her, I don't think, it was the conclusion I drew from it.

"What am I compared to Robert Grant, will you tell me? He's just my age but he's going around the world to look for his father, who's an adventurer, but here I am sick in bed because I'm jealous of him!"

"It's a book, Michel, it's just a made-up story, you can't be jealous of that!"

"I know it's just a made-up story, I'm not stupid! But ... But I'm sure there are little boys with that kind of father! I wish my father was an adventurer! And I wish I had to travel all over the world to find him! Papa's really nice but he's a printer, so he prints! It's all he knows how to do! He comes home Friday night with his Sacred Heart calendars or an ad for Cashmere Bouquet soap and he wants us to be thrilled! But I couldn't care less about his Sacred Heart calendars! Even if they're well printed! And he wasn't even in the war like other people because he was deaf!"

"I forbid you to talk about your father like that! At least he's here! Some fathers didn't come home from the war! D'you think you'd be better off if he'd gone to the war and hadn't come back? And if he was an adventurer he'd never be here so you'd really have something to complain about!"

"If he wasn't here I could ... I don't know, I could imagine what he was like and where he was, I could dream about him coming back and I'd wait for him, if I couldn't afford to go chasing after him ... And when he did come back, for sure it wouldn't be calendars that he'd be showing me!"

I was on the verge of tears. My mother took the three volumes of Jules Verne, piled them on her lap, and set the empty soup bowl on top of them.

"If Jules Verne puts ideas like that in your head, young man, you'll be going back to the Comtesse de Ségur, let me tell you."

"Mama, this makes twice that you've taken this book away from me! You can't stop me from finishing it! You're always telling me, if you start a book you have to finish it!"

"Not books that put crazy ideas in your head!"

She pulled up the covers, ran her hand through my soaking-wet hair.

"Anyway, no more reading till you're better. It doesn't make sense, being out of your mind like that over a book! You're lucky to have the father you've got and I hope you'll realize it one of these days! And I don't want to hear one more word, understand? I'm not punishing you, I'm doing you a favour! Now rest—that's what you need."

I'd got to the third volume, the most thrilling one, and I quite simply couldn't imagine never knowing how *Captain Grant's Children* ended. I suspected that Robert Grant would find his father—but where? And how? I told my mother that, moaning a little to make her feel sorry for me. She straightened her apron and said:

"You can ask Jacques to tell you how it ends. I'm sure he read it when he was little, he's read everything. And it didn't drive him crazy. Your brother had a head on his shoulders when he was twelve, not like some people ... "

Towards the end of the afternoon, after a dreamless nap that had perked me up a lot, I found the three volumes of *Captain Grant's Children* beside me on the covers. And a little note, in block letters. My mother hadn't gone to school for very long and she didn't write very often.

"I guess the end won't make you any crazier than you already are. And you can ask your great adventurer Robert Grant if anyone brings him hot chicken soup when he's got a fever!"

***

My parents must have discussed it all in secret because the following Saturday morning, right after the "weekend pancakes," the thick, soft, runny ones my mother made on Saturday or Sunday because my father adored them, but that made the rest of us a little sick to our stomachs because we ate too many, Papa put his hand on my shoulder and led me out onto Mont-Royal Street without saying a word.

I've already used the anecdote that follows in a 1981 play, *Remember Me*. I hope that anyone who knows the play, when they learn the origin of it, will forgive me for repeating it here.

When a child realizes that his parents aren't perfect, that his mother is no longer the most beautiful or the youngest, that his father isn't a hero, it's always a shock and hard to get used to. During childhood, we both admire and hate our parents, who seem to know so much while we know nothing, and they represent the highest form of authority while we have none; in adolescence, though, after our idols' clay feet are revealed, we try not to despise them as we go on loving them because we've finally learned how to love them intelligently, but it's hard; our critical sense is being developed and they are the first victims of it. I could say that I was in the early stages of that second phase as I walked along Mont-Royal Street with my father that morning in 1954. Because of a book I'd read, I was sliding, willingly and fairly quickly, towards contempt.

I was looking at Papa in profile: still upright but with a well-established belly and hair that was starting to get seriously thin, still alert, but more and more breathless when he climbed up stairs too quickly, and a tic in his right hand because of a pinched nerve in his palm. The doctor had told him that if he didn't have an operation his hand would close completely, that the day could come when he couldn't use it at all. But he didn't have the money for an operation. He was a good man and I adored him; I sometimes had the time of my life with him, as I described in *Twelve Opening Acts*; he had a heart of gold and was a loving husband and father, though he was sometimes remote because of his deafness, but that day, to me, he had the serious flaw *of not being Captain Grant*. He waved to the men and tipped his hat when a woman went by. Those purely civilized gestures that I'd always seen him make were beginning to get on my nerves, most likely because at the age of twelve, we want to go unnoticed. He had with him his lemon-yellow kid gloves, the ones for special occasions, which he did something strange with: he put on just one and kept the other folded in his hand so he could shake hands with any important people he might run into, or so he claimed. Another opportunity for my nascent contempt to show itself in a particularly nasty way: I was sure my father had never met a single important person in his life! In my opinion he'd wasted generations of right-hand gloves, the leather turning black to no avail.

We were walking east along Mont-Royal, which was unusual because the interesting shops and stores where most people went were located west of Papineau.

But something new had just opened at the corner of Bordeaux and Mont-Royal and I realized with amazement that we were heading there. Just next to the Mont-Royal convent, where on Sunday night I would see limousines from Outremont or Westmount dropping off bunches of chic and snobbish young girls coming back from a fancy weekend, Steinberg's, the brand-new chain of grocery stores, had just opened the most modern, the cleanest, most air-conditioned, colourful, and best-stocked food store anywhere on Plateau Mont-Royal. All the local housewives had been quick to take advantage of the opening bargains and to taste, with appreciative little cries, bits of sausage, cheese curds, stuffed olives or slices of pâté sitting on Ritz crackers broken in two. They felt as if they were stuffing themselves at Monsieur Steinberg's expense so they bought more, as much to thank him for feeding them as to encourage him in his new business.

Steinberg's was a very young company in 1954, I think, and we'd never seen so much food in one place. The owners of corner grocery stores complained, crying scandal at the cut prices, but housewives ignored them and spent hours gleaning in the enchanted domain of their new benefactor, Monsieur Steinberg, who sold them everything and more for less, and on top of it all, in a beautiful, modern, air-conditioned store.

My father hadn't yet set foot inside Steinberg's and I wondered why he, who hated grocery-shopping more than anything, was taking me there on a Saturday morning.

A din made up of metal shopping carts clattering across the tile floor, of conversations between neighbours that were deafening because the volume of the Muzak wasn't properly controlled, of announcements of bargains delivered through speakers by voices that weren't altogether familiar with their new medium, of brand-new cash registers that rang up the smallest sale in a peremptory way, in short, the cacophony produced by a new building that has yet to find its cruising speed, as Jules Verne might have said, hit us the minute the automatic doors opened before us (my father, like anyone else going there for the first time, had raised his arm to push open the doors, which had already opened by themselves, then looked around to make sure no one had seen him, especially me), but I knew that Papa didn't hear any of it and I let him guide me down aisles overloaded with foods of all kinds and household products, most of which were still unknown to us.

What was most amazing was that he seemed to know exactly where he was going! He headed straight for the canned goods, looked for the soups, stopped, bent down so he'd be at my height, and gripped my shoulder. He smelled of the Yardley Lotus cologne I'd given him for Father's Day and I decided that next year, I'd give him a different one.

He cleared his throat before he started.

"See those cans of Campbell's soup?"

"Uhuh ... "

"Now listen to me ... Those Campbell's soups are all the same colour, right, the same red on all the cans ... "

"Uhuh ... "

"Well, that's because of me."

"What do you mean, because of you?"

"Well, it's like this. When they print the labels that go around the cans, they have to be sure it's always the same red ... "

"Uhuh ... "

"See, there's a secret ... Now listen ... So the red will always be the same on every label, there's a secret recipe for Campbell's red ... a mixture of different printers' inks that's a deep, dark secret ... In every city in North America where they print those Campbell labels, there's *one* pressman in *one* print shop that knows the secret ... and here in Montreal, that man is your father! I've had that recipe for Campbell's red in my head for years, and I can't ever make a mistake, because if I did there'd be some labels not so red, some labels more pink, too pale, too dark ... and it would be my fault! Can you picture that, shelves full of Campbell's soups that had labels with all kinds of different reds? But they know they can count on me, that here in Montreal there won't be even one can of Campbell's soup that isn't the same red as the others!"

He straightened up, clearing his throat because he'd let himself go a little and become a little emotional as he spoke.

"Maybe I haven't gone around the world, Michel, but I've got a very big responsibility right here in Montreal and I'll *never* fail in my duty!"

He walked away, proud as a peacock, his head in the new fluorescent lights, his kid glove carefully folded in his left hand.

I ran to catch up with him and took his hand, though for years I hadn't let anyone hold my hand in public.

So much for Captain Grant!

***

That afternoon, my friend Réal Bastien, with whom I spent most of my free time when I wasn't reading, had followed me to Steinberg's under protest.

"I went there with my mother this morning, the last thing I want to do is go back now!"

"C'mon, I wanna show you something, you won't be sorry!"

I pushed him in front of the rows of hundreds of cans of Campbell's soup and shouted so everyone could hear me:

"Look at that! It's my father that invented Campbell's red!"

**

Had Papa lied to me? Had he made up that story in the face of the contempt I was beginning to show him, or quite simply to put an end to the crisis brought on by my reading *Captain Grant's Children*? I never wanted to know. I chose to believe him and I still do.

The telephone is right beside me. I could call one of my brothers, ask him if our father ever printed even one Campbell's soup can label, but where would that get me? If he confirmed the story, I'd feel guilty because I'd doubted Papa's word; if he denied it, I'd never get over it.

The Brothers Grimm

I must have checked out every version of *Snow White and the Seven Dwarfs* before I was ten years old.

Too often, we forget that for a child, the original version by the Brothers Grimm is much more terrifying than, let's say, the Walt Disney movie in which everything is pretty and innocent. You'll tell me that his wicked witch is terrifyingly ugly, but she appears to enjoy being ugly, seems not to take herself seriously, while in the Brothers Grimm description, she is *truly* ugly and *truly* wicked! Uncle Walt, easy-going American that he was, outrageously betrayed the German folk legend by turning the dwarfs into a troop of jolly fellows who yodel their little hearts out, accompanying themselves on the accordion or the pedal organ when they come home at nightfall from mining diamonds that were already cut to finish the day in their adorable little cathedral-roofed Swiss chalet. Nearly all the other versions are less bland and more menacing and have, when you think about it, a highly pernicious sexual connotation. One woman, seven men—imagine the parties in that house!

And what about the wicked witch, to get back to her, who disappears rather conveniently from the film, thrown from a mountain-top, but in the original version is condemned to dance *in white-hot metal shoes* till death ensues! Believe me, that leaves a permanent mark on a seven- or eight-year-old mind with the slightest imagination!

But that's not why I devoured every version of the story I could find. It was because of the ending, which quite literally hurt me. Though the books might differ on various aspects of how the story developed, the end was always desperately the end: no sooner had the dwarfs got used to Snow White's presence in their house (though it had been designed for small people), to the importance the princess was assuming in their lives (she quickly became a servant, at their service, in spite of her fancy education, obviously, who fed them, cleaned up after them, took care of their leisure activities when evening came, but misogyny in fairytales isn't what this story is about), than the wicked witch arrived on the scene with that apple of hers, and with Snow White knocked out, that big jerk of a Prince Charming shows up to kiss her more or less on the mouth, the way you kiss the auntie with the beard. The princess awakens, swoons before the young squire, they get married and live happily ever after. End of story.

And what about the poor dwarfs?

When I took out another version of *Snow White* from the children's room of the Municipal Library, the librarian—I ended up adoring her because she let me take out more books than I was really allowed—frowned.

"Another one? Aren't you sick of reading the same story all the time?"

"I haven't read this version though ... "

"So what do you expect? That the prince won't come and Snow White dries up in her glass coffin like a rotten old apple?"

I wasn't going to confess that I was actually dreaming that the survivor and the jerk would take the dwarfs along on their honeymoon, so I kept quiet. But every version of the tale, illustrated or not, long or short, in a small book or a big one with pictures, ended the same way, and it left me brooding and disappointed, curled up like a cat in my cabin of cushions.

Our living room sofa—an old thing that had been wine-red cut velvet during its better days, but that had ended up looking like a huge battered animal lying on its side—was where I holed up to read. I'd got in the habit of taking three cushions—two for the walls, one for the roof—to make myself a shelter where I felt safe even when I was reading the terrifying stories I'd already started to adore, that haunted my nights till the end of my adolescence. I called it "my magic cave," and I spent hours there daydreaming, reading or listening to the radio—"Big Sister," "Jeunesse dorée" or "Francine Louvain," if I happened to come down with the flu in the middle of winter.

To get back to the dwarfs, every version of the tale left them on their doorstep, heads hanging and hats in hand, while our heroes disappeared into the sunset without even turning around to wave them one last goodbye. What a nerve that Snow White had! And so ungrateful! After all, they'd taken her into *their* house when the wicked queen's messenger boy came running after her to tear her heart out! All right, she'd paid for her room and board by doing their housework, but they had saved her life! *And they loved her!* I couldn't understand how wishy-washy Prince Charming, whom she'd never laid eyes on before (except in the movie, where he arrives at the beginning to sing a stupid song beneath her balcony while she wriggles and squirms like an idiot), would be enough to make Snow White drop everything and everyone, with no regrets and no remorse.

Trying to imagine how dull the evening would be for the seven dwarfs after their love had gone brought on my first anxiety attacks. It was horrible! Surely they weren't going to yodel and dance like little lunatics without Snow White to accompany and urge them on when they started to flag (after all, they'd been digging up diamonds all day)! That's what a broken heart must be like: to have to go on doing everything the way you'd done before while the world is crumbling around you ... I curled up in my magic cave, hugged the book, and made up different endings for *Snow White and the Seven Dwarfs*.

***

The Guérin, the Jodoin, and the Beausoleil backyards were separated by wooden fences that were easy to climb over, which made a huge playground for us, rough but pleasant, dominated by the Jodoin's' tree, one of the tallest on the street, which became the goal when we played hide-and-seek or tag across the Fabre Street lane between Mont-Royal and Gilford. We did everything there: parades with, sometimes, religious themes—I'd curse because I had to play St. Joseph much too often—aborted plays that were never actually put on because squabbles always broke out before the day of the performance, cabins built out of any old thing that held together any old way, terrific games that invariably ended in tears because the girls would beat the boys and the guys were cry-babies, pissing contests among the boys, other more subtle and, in particular, odorous games, really rotten tricks such as making someone, preferably a girl, drink pee from a green bottle, claiming it was 7-Up, which were rarely punished because they were rarely denounced.

There were fourteen of us: three Guérins (Gisèle, Micheline, Pierrette); four Jodoins (Jean-Paul, Jean-Pierre, Marcelle, Serge); four Beausoleils (Nicole, Roger, Claude, a girl whose name I've forgotten); two Rouleaus (Ginette, Louise); and me, a knot of noisy children who spent the summer in the city because their parents couldn't afford anything else and who hollered from morning till night, good weather or bad, disguised or not, scorching heat or not.

An unwavering friendship united us and we would stay friends when my family moved to Cartier Street during the 1950s, unable as I was to form a new gang for myself in a neighbourhood I didn't know and that seemed threatening.

On blistering hot summer evenings, exhausted from playing frenetically when our mothers recommended reading and lemonade, we got together around the Beausoleils' swings to sing the most precious jewels from the Abbé Gadbois' collection, *La Bonne Chanson*. Our voices, most of them out of tune—especially mine—rose up into the humid Montreal night to howl the adventures of "The Little Shoemaker" or to describe the dramatic crossing of the boat in "Il était un petit navire" until Madame Beausoleil came out to tell us to be quiet because it was late and the neighbours were threatening to call the police, which wasn't true. Reluctantly we would break the shell that had enclosed us all day, I'd walk home with the Rouleau sisters, who lived next door to us, then go inside to the safety of my magic cave and read for a while before I went to sleep. Those summers were totally wonderful and I can still conjure up their exact tastes and smells.

One rainy summer when I was eleven or so, when it was absolutely impossible to play in the lane for more than an hour or two at a stretch because of the downpours, I got the idea of trying out my new ending for *Snow White* on my friends; on one particularly sodden afternoon, I offered to tell them a wonderful story.

The others didn't agree right away, some hating to sit still and listen to a story, others frankly doubting my ability to tell one.

Madame Beausoleil, who had heard me through her wide-open kitchen window, came bursting out of her house.

"You aren't going to tell indecent stories in my backyard, Michel Tremblay!"

"I don't want to tell indecent stories!"

"You just said you want to tell stories ... "

"Sure, but they're stories ... stories like you read in books, I mean like fairy tales, things like that ... "

"You're sure?"

"Sure I'm sure!"

"They aren't dirty stories that'll give my children ideas?"

"No ... I don't even know any dirty stories!"

"I'm not so sure!"

"You don't believe me?"

"Look me in the eye and tell me again, just to see ... "

Which I did, hoping she wouldn't see anything.

"Anyway. I can hear everything through my kitchen window, you know, and if I hear one word that isn't proper, you'll go straight home and you'll never set foot here again! Understand?"

"Yes ... Don't get mad, Madame Beausoleil ... And you can listen all you want, I don't mind!"

Actually I was rather flattered to be doing my act in front of an adult. But all fourteen of us were a little shocked to find out that she was spying on us in the middle of the day while she was cooking or doing her laundry ... The silliness she must have heard in a day, poor woman!

My first steps as a storyteller were far from triumphant. I got off to a bad start and nearly couldn't start at all.

"You know the story of *Snow White and the Seven Dwarfs?*"

A chorus of protests, catcalls, jeers.

"Not that!"

"That's so stupid!"

"Is *that* your wonderful story?"

"We know it by heart!"

"Anybody can tell that story!"

"It's for babies!"

"Let's play hide-and-go-seek, even if it's raining!"

I was dismayed. I hadn't even started and already they didn't understand me!

"Listen, it's not the story of Snow White I want to tell you."

"That's what you said though!"

"No it's not, I just asked if you know it!"

"Sure we know it, we aren't ignoramuses!"

"It's the first story my mother ever told me, when I was little!"

"And it's a stupid story!"

"And boring!"

"It's for babies!"

I put up my hand to silence them.

"And the ending never bothered you?"

"The ending?"

"What ending?"

"The ending of the story ... "

"Stories all end the same way, don't you know that?"

Thirteen little mocking voices, thirteen grimacing little faces, thirteen little darts in my over-sensitive heart.

"They get married and have lots of children!"

More laughter.

After glancing at the kitchen window, Nicole Beausoleil leaned over to us, lowering her voice.

"My mother says it's no picnic, having lots of children ... "

Marcelle Jodoin sighed.

"Mine says Snow White shouldn't've got married ... "

Micheline Guérin made a face.

"My grandmother doesn't even want me to read that story ... She says a woman in a house with seven men isn't respectable ... "

"But you just said it was a story for babies ... "

"I think it's a story for babies, it's my grandmother that says it isn't respectable!"

"Come on, let's play hide-and-go-seek! Last one out is a rotten egg!"

Serge Jodoin, one of the youngest in the group, runs off, climbs the fence, jumps into the Jodoin's' backyard, touches the maple tree. We can hear his little voice through the rain:

"Home free! I win!"

No one follows him; he comes back, looking pitiful.

"You big kids are mean! You never want to play!"

I try to restore peace but the youngest kids are pulling at each other, the older ones can't separate them, and I can see the time coming when I'll have to give up any urge to tell them my own personal ending for *Snow White and the Seven Dwarfs*.

But Ginette Rouleau, as usual, manages to restore order in the wet backyard; the younger kids are separated, the older ones sitting on the gallery chairs, the girls have straightened their dresses, the boys have pulled up their pants.

"We'll give him a chance. Let him talk, and if it's too boring we'll play charades."

I felt they weren't taking me seriously. Talk of replacing me with charades! Honestly!

I started slowly so they wouldn't get too confused. What I was about to tell them was fairly complicated and I myself was worried about getting lost in my own story.

"Okay, listen: remember how Snow White and Prince Charming go away right after Snow White wakes up in her coffin?"

"Sure!"

"You didn't expect them to stay there!"

"It was way too small! Little beds, little plates, little knives and forks ... "

"And little tiny toilets!"

"Okay, okay! Which means that the seven dwarfs had to stay all by themselves ... "

"Whaddya mean? They were by themselves before Snow White got there, weren't they?"

This wasn't going to be easy. I took a deep breath and got right to the heart of the matter.

"But see, what they forget to say in the movie and the books is that Prince Charming forgot the wedding ring that had dropped down into the coffin while he was kissing Snow White ... "

"What! They couldn't get married without the ring! You have to have a ring or it doesn't count!"

Ginette Rouleau was also our etiquette specialist.

"There's more ... "

Heads were starting to turn in my direction and my heart was beating a little faster.

"So imagine that Prince Charming had also forgotten to tell the seven dwarfs ... "

"What? What?"

"What country he was the prince of!"

"Big deal!"

"What difference does that make?"

"So they find the ring when they're cleaning up the coffin ... "

"Yuck! Did it smell dead in there?"

"Serge! Settle down and listen to Michel! Either that or go home!"

"So when they find the ring ... they don't know where to deliver it!"

Ginette frowns and I could tell I was in trouble ...

"But he's a prince, he can just buy another one!"

The others agreed; I'd have to think fast.

"See, it was a ring that'd been passed on from father to son in that royal family for generations, so they couldn't get married without it! The prince's father had just died, he'd given him the ring just before and told him to go and look for the perfect woman and the prince finds Snow White!"

No objections. Relief.

Serge Jodoin stuck his finger in his nose and started digging, probably hunting for some treasure that he'd fiddle with for long minutes, eyes wide and mouth agape.

"So what do the little dwarfs do to try and find the prince?"

"See, they separate and every one of them goes and visits a country ... "

"What?"

"They do not!"

"Come on ... "

"They do so—and what I want to tell you about is their adventures!"

"What?"

"That's not true!"

"Come on!"

I had the attention of the thirteen children, Madame Beausoleil, with a straight pin in her mouth, had stuck her head out her window, and she was frowning. I could begin.

But Ginette Rouleau raised her finger. I'd never be able to start my story!

"'Scuse me, but who kept the ring?"

"Whaddya mean, who kept the ring?"

"Look, there were seven of them, they had to put the ring somewhere in case one of them found Snow White and her husband! I mean, they couldn't phone!"

"Listen, who's telling the story? I haven't even started yet and you're asking questions! We won't get very far if you keep interrupting like that!"

"If you take it like that I'm going home!"

"No, don't, stay here and let me start!"

I had to think fast and make up something, this time about the damn wedding ring which, yes, I'd forgotten about ... I started before I even knew how I was going to finish my sentence.

"And I'll have you know, sure I thought about the ring! (Think fast! Think fast!) So the ring ... about the ring ... they'd tied it to a rabbit's tooth and they shut the rabbit inside the house with tons of carrots and they told the rabbit to wait for them and never spit out the ring because it looked like he had a gold tooth and it suited him really well. Okay?"

Whew!

Ginette stood there gawking. She'd wanted to test me, I'd done brilliantly, now I had her confidence. I could take the plunge without fear.

My story so captivated my listeners that over the weeks that followed, good weather or bad, fifteen minutes a day were devoted to the adventures of the seven dwarfs on seven continents (Ginette, our geography champion, did question the number of continents, but I told her that the world of fairytales had some that we didn't know about, and to my great relief that seemed to satisfy her).

I didn't make up everything, far from it. I took my inspiration from what I was reading; from all the movies I'd ever seen; from the soap operas we listened to at home (I remember in particular that a series entitled "Flying Saucer S-52" came in handy when one of the dwarfs was kidnapped by creatures from another planet); from fairytales my girl-cousins had told me; from the ones Tante Lucille read on the radio Saturday morning; from the comics in *La Presse*; from the comics I bought from Monsieur Guimond on Gilford Street. I took my comical effects from *Zézette* and my dramatic ones from Charles Perrault or Hans Christian Andersen; I combined them all any old way, going from one dwarf to another when I ran out of inspiration. I brought in the good fairy from *Pinocchio*, the cruel stepmother from *Aurora, the Child Martyr*, the whale from *Moby Dick*, Puss in

Boots and Yvan l'intrépide, Peter Pan and Mickey Mouse, Hitler and Rin-Tin-Tin; I used what I'd remembered from the descriptions of Jules Verne, whom I'd just discovered; I mimicked, I put on different voices, I cried when somebody was about to die and I jumped up and down with excitement when two enemies were reconciled at last, after ten thousand years of complicated squabbles and bloody wars.

A broom became a sword and then a magic wand and then it went back to being the broom that belonged to a witch (for instance, the one who lost a tooth whenever she said, "J'ai frette!" instead of "J'ai froid!" when she was cold and who bragged that she'd lost over ten thousand!), then was transformed into a gigantic candy that one of the dwarfs poisoned to put some giant or other to sleep; I took towels off the clothesline to make robes for myself, underwear for hats, socks for ears. I became in turn a ballerina, a knight, a dragon, a polar bear, or an earthworm, trying to find a personality and a voice for each of the characters I invented. If it didn't work I'd switch dwarfs and pick up a story I'd abandoned days before, hoping that no one would realize it was all tied together with very strong rope.

But Ginette Rouleau was always there to put me back on the right path.

I wanted to kill her when she asked one of her rotten questions, but I always made it my duty to give her a satisfactory answer. Actually, I think she was my first critic!

I tried to imitate the American serials that got me so worked up in the parish hall on Saturday afternoon, and to leave one hero every day in danger of death or about to discover an important clue about the comings and goings of Snow White and that jerk, her husband. It was hard, but so fantastic when it worked!

My evenings were devoted to what I would tell them the next day, I often slept badly, I died of stage-fright before the day's performance—but I was happy.

Without realizing it, I was learning how to use my imagination, how to construct a story, and, most of all, how to make others love me by becoming indispensable. I was already learning how to be a form of entertainment!

I have no memory of how I ended my story, I'm not even sure that I did end it. Defeatist as I've always been, I was quite capable of deciding that after travelling for seven years across seven countries on seven continents, the seven dwarfs hadn't tracked down their idol, that they'd come home empty-handed and found instead of their pretty house, a sky-high mountain of rabbit turds!

Strangely enough, it never occurred to me that summer to write out the stories I was telling. I didn't yet feel any need to settle down at the dining room table where I did my homework and confide to the blank page; that would come later, when I started having personal problems to recount, I suppose, instead of adventures gleaned here and there and spiced up, only spiced up, by my imagination.

Summer sped by, we didn't mind the downpours, and I think that all fifteen of us, Madame Beausoleil included, were searching for Snow White and her insipid spouse.

***

"You haven't taken out a book about *Snow White and the Seven Dwarfs* for a while now ... Did you finally get sick of her?"

"No ... I never found the ending I wanted so I made up seven of my own."

A CHICKEN FOR CHRISTMAS

Jo Hatcher

The same librarian.

"Something's just come in that might interest you ... "

She disappears behind the back wall of the huge room where the new books are received, inventoried and labelled, the holy of holies to which I've never been admitted despite my tremendous curiosity. My heart beats faster. Has Captain Johns published a new adventure of Worrals or Biggles, has the "Collection Jean-François" finally brought out *La Tortue d'ébène,* the much-anticipated sequel to *Le Lac sans fond* that I've been asking for for months? Or maybe they've finally repaired the binding of the last volume of *The Scarlet Pimpernel,* which I hadn't read yet because it was so badly damaged?

She comes back with a booklet that hasn't yet been bound in stale-chocolate brown or sick green and holds it out to me with a look of complicity.

"You can borrow this even though it hasn't been catalogued yet. But I can't let you take it out, so you'll have to read it here ... It won't take you long. When I saw it I thought about you right away. I won't say why, I want you to figure that out by yourself ... "

So, a mystery!

What a let-down. The cover is pink. A girls' book! An incredibly banal title: *A Chicken for Christmas.* An author, a woman I've never heard of. An illustration that would put you off reading: a family around a table for what seems to be a Christmas meal as dreary as ours. We're a long way from Biggles' thrilling aerial battles or the stormy crossings of the English Channel by the Scarlet Pimpernel, enemy of the French revolution, that fascinated me so much at the time ...

I look up at the librarian, disappointed. She smiles.

"It's not so much the book itself ... Look, if you've got half an hour, sit at one of these tables and read it very carefully ... "

"The last *Scarlet Pimpernel* hasn't been bound yet?"

"No. But never mind the *Scarlet Pimpernel,* read this. Let me know what you think."

I'll do it to make her happy because nothing about the book appeals to me.

More pitiful than I'd want to appear (this isn't school after all, with required reading that's tiresome on top of everything), I go to one of the huge varnished tables. A few children are reading Tintin. I sit down with them—something I never do because for me, reading is a solitary pleasure—and open the book.

From the very beginning I know that this is one of the silliest books I've ever read. There's nothing interesting about the story, nothing surprising about the characters, nothing to say about the style because it's an insipid translation from the English; it's childish, it's babyish, I hate it ... The one virtue is that it's short, and since I have my back to the counter where the librarian sits enthroned, I skip some parts. I don't read the descriptions, just glance at them long enough so I can answer her questions, because I know that she'll have some, she lent me this book for a reason!

But what will I say when she asks if I liked it? Should I lie so I won't hurt her feelings?

And why was she so insistent? After all, she stamps the books I take out, she's known what I like for ages! Not one of the books I've taken out since I joined the Municipal Library five or six years ago is anything like this. Not one! I've got better taste than that.

I race through the rest of the booklet and close it. I don't dare turn around yet. If only she would take sick, if only an ambulance would come for her and she had to have an emergency operation, I wouldn't have to face her! I'm gathering my courage when my attention is drawn to what's written on the back of the book. In particular, a number, which makes me look more carefully. Thirteen. Thirteen years old ...

It's so shocking that I jump. This book, boring though it is, was written by a little girl of thirteen! A girl *my* age! A girl *my age* who managed to get a book published. A bad one, even!

I finish the brief story. London, England. In London, England, thirteen-year-old children can publish books!

I pick it up again, leaf through it, bury my nose in it. A beautiful brand new book that still smells of printers' ink!

And all done by a little girl! This book has made its way to me, at the other end of the world, deep in the heart of French Canada, where even the great writers—according to my brother Jacques, who has finished his classical studies and who knows everything—have trouble getting published because it costs so much! In school they teach us that we live in the land of paper and that the Europeans, who don't have much, are forced to buy it from us, but we can't publish our own writers. And people in England have bought paper from us to publish a thirteen-year-old! It's hard to believe.

I'm in such pain, my jealousy is so bitter that I start to cry like a baby. I've only barely started writing, for myself alone, very timid little things that I hide in my brother's big Atlas so no one will find them, I haven't dared to even dream of being published some day, because I never thought it would be possible, and now this English girl with no talent is giving me a complex! It's the true frustration of a budding writer that's making me react that way, the injustice it represents that amazes me: if I, at my age, wrote such a terrible book, would anyone in Montreal go to the trouble of publishing me? Here in the country of paper? Absolutely not! I come from a godforsaken French-speaking place that's drowned in a sea of English and the chances of my name being not *known* but simply *pronounced* in England are nil, totally nil! Not that I want to be known in England, the thought of it has never crossed my mind, needless to say, but for the first time in my life, I wish I were free enough to be able to dream about it! I want that dream, if I ever do have it, not to be irrevocably blocked just because I'm a French-Canadian! If that silly twit has been able to come to me, why don't I have the chance, the right, to go to her?

I cry harder and harder, my shoulders shaking, snot dripping from my nose, I haven't got anything to wipe it with because it's summer and in the summer you never have colds ... The humiliation for a thirteen-year-old of being obliged to wipe his nose on the sleeve of his flowered cotton shirt in front of everybody is indescribable. You want to die, no, worse, you're already dead!

The other children look at me, frowning. What's wrong with the dope that's crying over a girls' book?

Suddenly she's crouching beside me. Panicking. She hugs my shoulders, then my head; she holds me tight against her. I'm sure she smells good, like cleanliness and soap, but I can't smell a thing, my nose is plugged forever. I know I'm going to choke to death on my own snot and it'll be my own fault!

"My Lord, what's the matter? What's wrong with you? I did that ... I did it because I thought that maybe you had dreams of becoming a writer yourself some day, you're such a reader ... Why are you crying? I just wanted you to know that it's possible to get published even for someone very young ... "

I push her away, I get rid of her, I'm standing beside the oak table, furious, pointing an accusing finger at her, my voice quivering.

"Sure you can. In England!"

I hurl the book to the floor and walk out before she can say anything.

***

I'm slumped on a bench in Parc Lafontaine, looking across at the library, the cause of my frustration, my anger, and I hate it. I know I'll never set foot inside there again! What's the good of reading so many books if you can't even dream about publishing one some day!

Then I think about my Grandmother Tremblay, about Madame Allard, who have read so much, about my brother Jacques too, an inveterate reader, about my mother who devours big fat books in no time: have they ever dreamed of writing? I've never wondered about that, focussed as I was on my own budding desire.

But does reading necessarily lead to an urge to write, to a need to write?

For me, it's been true for some time now, but when others look at a page they think is particularly well-written, whether it's by Henry Bordeaux, Balzac, Pierre Benoit or George Sand—lately my brother has been swooning over *La Mare au diable*—have they ever dreamed, as I do more and more, that they were the writer, that they were living inside Balzac or George Sand, sitting in front of the beautiful blank page in a big notebook and *writing* with a passion that comes close to madness the story that they're reading?

My thoughts are muddled. Did my grandmother ever, just once in her life, dream of being Zola? Did my brother Jacques see himself sometimes as George Sand? Does everyone dream of being George Sand when they read her? Why not? Everyone has a story to write, a book to give birth to!

My grandmother in particular would have had such wonderful things to write down before she died! Her childhood in Charlevoix County, the four white boats that left from La Malbaie to sail up the Saguenay—the *Tadoussac*, the *Québec*, the *Saint-Laurent* and the *Saguenay*—I can still remember, and when I rhyme off their names I count them on my fingers, the way she showed me when I was a small child; Lac Saint-Jean at the very end, a dark inland sea so beautiful that she couldn't talk about it without taking out her handkerchief; how suffocated she'd felt when she was obliged to move to Montreal at the beginning of the century, to follow Télésphore Tremblay whom she was going to marry ... The misery, the black misery of the farmers all over Quebec who'd come to the city to become underpaid workers, "cheap labour" for the big English companies— they who had known nothing but the open air ... All the time when she was immersing herself in the nineteenth-century French or English or Russian peasantry, had she dreamed of putting down on paper her own genesis at the other end of the world? I wish so much that she were still here so I could ask her. ("Gramma, did you ever write books in your head?" "Yes I did, sweetie, and I want you to know, they were wonderful!")

Obviously, there's the question of talent. But who could have said, who could have judged whether she had any? Whether I have any? And is the need to express yourself stronger than the talent to do it? Is talent the only thing that gives people the right to express themselves?

For a few seconds I see the five of us sitting around the dining room table; I've resurrected my grandmother and Madame Allard, improved them a little, they don't limp now, their feet under the table are perfectly straight—my mother and my brother have their noses in their work, pens are scratching at paper; now and then someone sighs or laughs contentedly because they've just completed a fine sentence. The satisfaction of a job well done. The right word. The right formula. Finally, Madame Allard and my grandmother talk to each other, softly so they won't disturb the other writers. What they say must be very beautiful, because they're wiping their eyes with lace handkerchiefs. Now and then my mother hums "Le Temps des cerises," the song that has been with her all her life. I cry for the second time in less than half an hour but this time, I'm euphoric. Ah! To spend the rest of my life in their company, nestled between Mama and Grandma, who've been made eternal by my will alone, and write!

Unrealistic dream! Stupid idiot! You'd have to move to England!

***

"I'm glad you came back. I confess, I was worried when you left like that ... I even phoned your mother."

I'd like to tell her where to go. I restrain myself.

"I just came to tell you I'm cancelling my membership."

She takes off her glasses, which hang around her neck from a gold chain. It's the first time I've seen such a thing and I lose my concentration. She leans over towards me.

"You don't have to cancel anything, just stop borrowing books ... "

That's all. I wish that she'd tried to dissuade me, pleaded with me to stay, yelled at me because I'd've been glad to say no, but this cold indifference is surprising and disconcerting. So it means nothing to her to lose one of her most faithful borrowers? Or does she want me to go to her on my own, confide in her, confess? Well, she can wait! All I have to do now is turn on my heels and leave her with as much dignity as possible ... but I can't.

"You're jealous of the little English girl, aren't you?"

"No, I'm just not interested in reading any more."

She's trying not to smile, I can tell, and I'd like to rip off her glasses, throw them down and stamp on them. Then her little gold chain would be useless!

She's too perceptive, I don't want to see her again as long as I live!

"Anyway, if you change your mind ... "

I take back my library card which I'd left on the counter earlier.

And that's all. It's over. I'll never read again. I look around the room one last time. Farewell, my friends. I'm wallowing in my misery. I see myself standing in the middle of the room, bidding heart-rending farewells to Michel Strogoff and Worrals, and I think it would make a nice sad scene in a family-fare movie. I hope she feels sorry for me and that she'll regret her foul deed for the rest of her life, the old cow! Actually she's not old at all, but she's still a cow.

I head for the door.

"If you want an apology, if you want us to talk, you win ... I don't understand what happened, I'd like you to tell me ... "

I'm outside.

Will she come running after me, shout on the street that she was wrong, that she's *truly* sorry? I slow down.

Nothing.

Dammitall anyway!

***

A few days later I can't take it any more, I can't imagine one more day without reading and I go back to the library as if nothing had happened, and choose six books.

She says nothing, only stamps the cards a little more energetically than usual. And I have the strong impression that she's giving me a strange look. I pretend I don't notice.

In future, I'll try not to dream too much when I read. If I can.

WORRALS, BIGGLES, KING

Captain W.E. Johns

She had come rushing into the double room that served as a bedroom for my two brothers and me, a large space, decrepit but comfortable and pleasant, with a balcony looking down on the corner of Cartier and Mont-Royal.

My Grandmother Tremblay was dead, my Aunt Robertine and her son, Claude, had moved out, my father's brothers, Fernand and Gérard, were settled in a rooming house on Papineau, so we finally had an apartment to ourselves. It was expensive though, so to make ends meet, my parents rented a room, the first one on the right as you came inside, to a Monsieur Migneault, who was very nice but very fond of cologne.

As usual, I was reading.

"Michel, quit squirming like a caterpillar in that chair or I'll get out the Raid! If only I could dream that one day you'll turn into a butterfly!"

"I've already asked you to knock before you come into my room, Mama!"

"I'll knock on our boarder's door but let me tell you, buster, the day when I knock before I come in here, hens will have teeth and pigs will lay eggs!"

"I'm getting really fed up, I can't even get a little privacy!"

"You've got nothing to hide from your mother!"

Actually, like all teenagers I had plenty to hide from my mother, of which the fact that I'd started to play with myself while reading the novels of Captain W.E. Johns was not the least important. And need I add that I didn't want her barging in at the crucial moment? Which nearly happened, actually: I'd just had time to withdraw my hand when I heard her footsteps in the hallway. If my mother had been a thinner woman who walked more discreetly, she'd have caught me that day in mid-mortal sin. Probably I'd have died of shame. And so would she.

"And move your carcass, you have to go to Household Finance!"

"Again! Isn't that finished yet? I've been going there every Friday for practically a year!"

"That's right, and you'll be going for another six months! If you aren't interested in giving back the money we borrowed, you should've been born to a family with money! Meanwhile, like the man said, get up and walk. And I'd like to sit in *my* chair, if you don't mind ... "

Her chair was a wine-red leatherette monster from the first generation of La-Z-Boys, I think, that my brothers had bought her a few months earlier but that had ended up in our room because it was too bulky for my parents' room, or even for the dining room with the TV set. They'd given it to her so that she could rest comfortably while she was watching her favourite shows, but there wasn't room for it in the dining room and no question of moving the TV to our room, the only other large one in the apartment. But as they'd also just equipped our "bachelor pad" with an air-conditioner, at least Mama could enjoy the cool air while she took a break in her chair.

It was August and all that month, because of her weight and Montreal's unbearable humidity, my mother was impossible to get along with. She became irascible and impatient, constantly complaining, and she took out of mothballs the annual dose of caustic bad faith that could make her so obnoxious. We all understood how exasperated she was—it was one of the first facts of life that I'd learned: don't upset Mama during heat waves. We all walked on eggs, the house became a silent cloister where it was best not to run into the mother superior during her bad spells.

That year though, thanks to the armchair and the air conditioner, Mama spent her first nearly normal summer in a very long time, and we all blessed modern technology, even if it meant that she could show up in the middle of the night and stretch out in her La-Z-Boy for a few hours—I'd wake at dawn to go for a pee and find her there, lying on her back, offered up to sleep, snoring just enough to be reassuring. Or she could burst in unexpectedly at any moment of the day to oust me because, of course, I was the one who took advantage of it most.

Between orders from the nearby Ty-Coq Barbecue, where I'd been a delivery boy in my spare time for over a year, I'd go home to get comfortable and read—afternoons were fairly quiet and the owner, Monsieur Dubuc, let me leave during slack periods; so if she wanted to enjoy *her* chair, my mother had to dislodge me.

"If you want to use your La-Z-Boy, Mama, you don't have to send me to Household Finance, just ask and I'll sit somewhere else."

"If I want to use my La-Z-Boy, Michel, I don't even have to ask, I can just kick you out, or sit on you and flatten you if you don't move it!"

I thought she was probably having a bad day—which happened in spite of the new acquisitions—and that it was best to give her the chair, which was hers, after all.

I extricated myself with a sigh, the book flattened against my erection which refused to disappear.

"And let me see what you're reading ... I'd like to know what it is that keeps you inside on such a gorgeous day!"

I stuffed my hand in my pocket and handed her the book.

She had on one of those pale blue sleeveless cotton nighties that was the only thing she wore when it was too hot, that took me back to my early childhood, those blessed years when I could climb onto her, onto that mountain of warm, soft flesh, to beg for the affection she never refused me. Even in August. Now times had changed. The affection was still there, but it was shown in a different way. For some time now, when I became too loving with Mama, a certain brusqueness had replaced the warmth I'd known when I was little ... I probably didn't want to move away from childhood or her warmth, my mother sensed it, and she was doing her best to make me understand that a thirteen-year-old boy couldn't climb onto his mother and kiss her any more. Alas!

She stood with her back to the La-Z-Boy, leaned on its arms, bending over and bending her legs, backside in the air, gave herself a push towards the back, lay down with a shuddering sound as some air went out of the leatherette, arched her back a little to bring up the footrest. I'd seen her do it too often to think it was funny; now I found it touching. The operation always required a great effort and she'd have to get her breath back before she spoke.

"I'm making progress, I got it on the first try this time ... Sometimes I feel like I'm drowning in red leatherette! Okay, now where's that book?"

It had slipped down between her thigh and the arm of the chair. I fished it out and handed it to her.

"Here ... But you won't like it, it's war stories and battles in airplanes ... "

"Let me decide what I like or don't like, do you mind?"

"You're mean!"

"That's right, in August I'm mean, didn't you know that already?"

So much for conversation; she was pretending to read.

"Where's the money?"

"You'll find exactly two dollars and fifty cents on the kitchen table. And don't forget what I told you ... "

"You tell me every week, Mama; don't worry, I couldn't forget it if I wanted to!"

***

Those weekly visits to Household Finance were the shame of my mother. And mine. Mama hid from my father and brothers the fact that she borrowed money, I was forced to be her accomplice because I was the one who repaid the loan, a little at a time, and that role, which I'd enjoyed at first—it was one more secret that I shared with her—had finally upset me when I discovered the reasons: the pride of that woman who'd always been poor and who now, when her husband and sons were beginning to be able to spoil her, preferred to go to a finance company rather than ask them for money; that unhealthy need to seem to be someone who balances her budget and can treat herself to all sorts of useless things when actually the money came from Household Finance; that pride which led her to parade to Sunday Mass in extravagant hats that had cost a lot but hadn't been paid for ...

One of my greatest frustrations is that I wasn't able to spoil her as she deserved because she passed away too soon, wasn't able to shower her with gifts until she could say for once in her life: "I don't want any more, I've got enough!" My brothers, much older than me, had known the pleasure of seeing her bring her hand to her heart and exclaim: "That wonderful La-Z-Boy! You shouldn't have, I don't deserve it ... " I too, because my name was always there, after Armand, Jacques and Bernard, but it was just a formality, I was too young to share expenses with them. I was merely there, a helpless spectator and not one of the actors, and I'll regret it as long as I live.

Today, she would be ninety-two and she'd be the most contented old lady in the world.

I'd got to know Household Finance very early. Just weeks before my first communion, mamma had taken me by the hand, walked to the branch on Mont-Royal Street, and shown me to the manager as an indisputable alibi, saying:

"I need a hundred dollars. It's for him. For his first communion. For his clothes and the party."

I had the nicest suit and the nicest party in the parish, but Mama had gone to the Household Finance office once a week for two years to pay for them.

The branch was nearby, above the Woolworth's on Mont-Royal between Papineau and Cartier; I just had to go a few hundred steps to get there. But a very strict code had been established for those visits, a precise itinerary that I must never depart from: no one could ever see me going in there and I had to behave in such a way that no one knew about my visits to Household Finance. Always.

It was no small undertaking, because as a BBQ chicken delivery boy I was very well-known in the neighbourhood; all the salesmen and saleswomen on Mont-Royal, especially my customers, called me Ty-Coq and waved when I went past their shops. How could I go unnoticed?

It's always in mid-afternoon, when the sidewalks on Mont-Royal Street are nearly deserted. Mama hands me two dollars and fifty cents, offers me the same instructions that I know by heart, gives me a push because I don't want to go. I walk down the stairs of 4505 Cartier Street, turn onto Mont-Royal for a hundred feet or so, checking carefully to make sure that no salesmen or saleswomen are looking out at the street. If someone says hello, if someone waves, I have to pretend to be shopping, that's the order I've been given. Luckily for me, right beside the finance company's office there's a very small bookstore. It sells mainly practical books that don't interest me at all, but it's an alibi that's not to be scorned: everybody knows that I like to read, so no one notices if I stand there a little too long with my nose against the window, reading the titles of books on angling or building birdhouses. When my breath leaves too much mist on the glass in the winter, I move a few inches and start over, though I've had more than enough time to read every title on display. I have to wait till there's *nobody* in sight on Mont-Royal between Cartier and Papineau and *all* the salespeople in the shops across the street are busy serving customers or putting things away before I move ... The wait is sometimes hard on my nerves. I think I must look like a thief getting ready to act: while I feign interest in the window displays, I keep turning my head to see if anyone's coming. If I've had time to check out both windows twice before the opportunity arises to climb up the inside staircase to Household Finance, I'll repeat the routine at Woolworth's. But it's kind of embarrassing for an teenager to stand for five minutes in front of a transparent nylon négligée or a display of cotton brassieres ... A thief and a pervert! When I'm *absolutely* sure that I'm safe, I duck my head and charge ... All this has to be done at lightning speed. Above all, not give anyone time to turn the corner or to look up at me.

That day though, because of the humidity and heat, Mont-Royal Street was empty and I was able to go up to the HFC office fairly quickly. The inhabitants of Plateau Mont-Royal had better things to do than walk on sticky pavement or overheated sidewalks.

Always the same blonde lady behind her counter. (But wasn't she "somebody" too?) She could tell all, denounce us to anyone. (Then again, maybe she'd sworn an oath ...) Still the same contemptuous look at the member of the masses who's come with his weekly two dollars and a half. Open the little notebook, subtract the amount, stamp the little notebook, close it. Bye, see you next week, poor boy! I often felt like asking her how much she got paid to sneer at me like that, but I never did because I must not, for any reason, attract attention to myself.

But when I turned around to go back down the old stairs, shoot!, it's Madame Pilozzi, our landlady! A moment of terror for me, embarrassment for her. A look of recognition between poor people who use the same expedient to survive. And my father always says that with the eighty dollars a month they get for our apartment, the Pilozzis must be rich! Too big a mortgage maybe, or delusions of grandeur like my mother ... After this incident I could never run into Madame Pilozzi on the inside stairs of the house on Cartier Street without thinking of the moment of horror that had brought us together. A little hesitation-waltz, after you, no, no, you go first, a little nod, pounding heart, the staircase ten times longer than usual, Mont-Royal Street too stifling hot ... Oh God, I forgot to look down before I went out, maybe somebody saw me! Maybe *two* people know our secret!

***

"You certainly took your time!"
  "It was ages before I could go in ... "
  "Nobody saw you?"
  "No, nobody saw me go in ... "
  "Are you sure?"
  "Mama, I told you—nobody saw me go in!"
  (Quick, change the subject ...)
  "Did you start the book?"
  "Yes. I don't see why you said I wouldn't like it ... I love those war stories! I'm telling you, the action on just one

page ... And one of the characters is French-Canadian! Can I borrow it before you take it back to the library?"

"Okay. But you'll have to read it tonight because I have to return it tomorrow."

"For heaven's sake, even if it takes me another day it won't kill you!"

"I absolutely have to take back the books tomorrow, Mama, I'm out of things to read!"

"Out of things to read! The house is full of books ... "

"I've read them all."

"Michel, don't tell me you've read *all* the books in the house!"

"They were my books when I was little, I know them by heart."

"I see you digging around in your brother's books ... I'm sure you haven't read all of those."

"No, because you won't let me, you say that they're about women whose husbands cheat on them and lovers and mistresses and they're too old for me ... Are you going to let me read them now? Because if you are, I won't ever have to go back to the library!"

"Don't argue with me this afternoon, I'm not in the mood! I told you you could look at those books when you're sixteen and you're going to wait till you're sixteen! And you're going to give me time to read that Captain Johns! If you want to read, you can read the backs of the Corn Flakes boxes and that's that! The world won't come to an end if you go half a day without reading, you know! When you're blind, buster, you'll see that I was right but it will be too late. And in the meantime, while you can still see, give me a hand, I have to make supper ... It's all very well to like reading, but I've got four elephants that have to be fed. When you're a keeper in a zoo you have to take the troubles that go with it!"

She's smiling as she leaves the room, pleased with her last tirade, admirable in her conviction that she's the indisputable queen of the well-constructed monologue and the funny and well-placed insult. I was smiling too. In a few sentences she'd outlined quite precisely what she thought of me, she was well aware that I'd enjoyed her performance and I got the message—"Touch just one of your brother's books and you'll wish you were dead!"—and she made her way majestically to her stove and saucepans.

I plunged back gladly into Captain Johns' novel.

I'd already read at least a hundred, devouring them the way that later on, I would devour Agatha Christie or Maurice Leblanc, in one sitting, sprawled in the belly of the wine-red monster whose leatherette was warm in winter, cool in summer, totally cut off from the rest of the world, immersed to the point of drowning in the adventures of Worrals, Biggles and King.

In that indescribably ugly chair I spent years experiencing what I was reading with a passion, a conviction, a concentration that sometimes made me ill. It was there that I lost the Trojan War, by choice because I never thought much of the Greeks and their unbearable pretentiousness, I was fascinated by the House of Atreus though I didn't like them, preferring the Trojans who were more civilized and more cultivated, the brave Hecuba over the hysterical Clytemnestra, the wise Priam over the arrogant Agamemnon, the love of art over the love of war. I flew above London along with Wendy Darling, even if I was too old, because I kept going back to *Peter Pan*, especially when I began to seriously refuse to become an adult (a man, actually). There too, I tried to solve my first whodunits, but the divine Agatha was always more Machiavellian than I was, inevitably leaving me speechless with admiration. And it was in that chair too that I detested Maigret, with his annoying cases of the flu and his smelly pipes, though I adored the novels that were so human; that I read my last Jules Verne, my first Saint-Exupéry, my last Féval, my first

97

Dostoevsky, my last Trilby, my first de Beauvoir, my last Baroness Orszy, my first Baudelaire, my last in the "Signe de Piste" collection, my first NRF title. It was there that I marked the end of my childhood with Rimbaud, and launched my adulthood with Oscar Wilde's *Portrait of Dorian Gray*.

Mama used to say that I was growing up lying down in a La-Z-Boy and that one fine day I'd wake up with wine-red leatherette skin and fatal bedsores. But I came out of it, having become an adult through reading that was often too serious for my age, with my skin paler and more sensitive than ever and incurable wounds to my soul.

And so I plunged back with rapture into the adventures of Captain Lorrington King, known as Gimlet, of the famous Commando to *King's Kitten*, while I fiddled with a cigarette burn that one of my brothers, probably Jacques, who spent more time there than Bernard, had accidentally made in the arm-rest. I have a very clear memory of that hole, which I couldn't stop touching, rubbing, scratching, depending on how excited I was from my reading; if the vile Nazi, von Zoyton—*the* bad guy in the novels of Captain Johns, who reappeared from book to book, chasing all the author's heroes, as often King as Worrals or Biggles—if he made someone suffer in a particularly depraved way or came out with one of those bold lines that gave me the shivers ("You vill remember fon Zoyton for ze rhest uff your days!"), the cigarette burn would feel the effects and bits of wine-red leatherette would be pulled, rolled, pinched and finally snipped off between the nails of thumb and forefinger. When I read poetry or psychological novels, the hole stayed more or less intact; but if I was reading an adventure novel as I was on that day, or a detective novel, the hole would grow appreciably and I could already hear my mother call out as she settled into it:

"If you don't stop stretching that hole in the leather you'll be missing a left hand!"

I'm quite sure that I read *all* of Captain Johns's books between the ages of twelve and fourteen, all that were in the Municipal Library collection at least. I'd devour them in a few hours, excited and feverish, ignoring the implausible, the doubtful coincidences, the sometimes botched endings; I hunted Nazis sitting next to Biggles, the number one pilot in British aviation; I admired the composure of King, whom nothing seemed to move or bother in the least; I regaled myself on the humour of Worrals, the brave and inventive KWAC with whose assistant, the aptly named Freckles, she was perhaps in love. To my great surprise, let me add.

Worrals and Freckles are the first two characters in books who made me suspect the existence of lesbianism. By that time I had accepted, understood and named my own leanings, in every book I read I searched for characters who shared my tastes, but needless to say, I never found any, because books for children were totally devoid of them and just when I was starting to wonder if the same thing existed for women, along came Worrals and Freckles, probably not lesbians at all, but their mutual affection, their rather surprising profession—both were pilots—their somewhat virile humour and their constant victories over the evil von Zoyton made me think that they weren't ordinary women and that just maybe, the female sex also ...

I analyzed every sentence of the novels they appeared in, every word they said, especially their jokes, in search of the slightest clue; eventually I found some, thanks to some intellectual gymnastics and risky suppositions and, I confess, I was a little jealous of them. I tried to imagine what went on *after* the novel was finished—my *Snow White* syndrome again—what they might say or do to each other once the adventure was over, von Zoyton defeated, the airplane parked in its garage; my solar plexus became all warm, but my hand did not yet leave the hole in the wine red leatherette ...

What is surprising is that I didn't find the same loaded contents in the novels about Biggles or King. With time, I'd given up on Worrals, because it was too easy to steer her away from her heterosexual trajectory, and *introduced* into Captain Johns's other novels material that I didn't find in them. I added my own homoerotic content and my vision of that world of men at war, who weren't risking anything because they were fictional heroes and we knew in advance that they'd emerge victorious from their adventures, changed completely. With Worrals my curiosity won out; with the male characters, it was my entire being that participated, with a lack of constraint that was totally new.

The people around King, in particular, were victims of that.

As King had three assistants, the youngest of whom was a French-Canadian trapper whose name resembled mine—he was called "Trapper" *Troublay*, which was convenient—I could easily identify with him and I could in perfect security, hidden inside Trapper Troublay, fall in love with my chief, who was so kind, so generous, so brave. Especially because the trapper in question was the most discreet of King's Kittens, speaking in monosyllables, always claiming to agree with everything King said or did. I moved around my idol then with total impunity, because I knew that he'd never be aware of my feelings. As well, he freed me when I was a prisoner, thanked me when I was the one who'd saved his life, rather effusively despite his usual coolness, he assigned me tasks that were delicate and difficult, and was generous with pats on the back and sincere compliments: what more could one ask of one's hero? One's Eros?

When King spoke to Trapper Troublay to give him orders or just to make conversation, when he actually deigned to acknowledge his existence, I slipped my hand furtively inside my pants and my imagination, all psyched up, quickly spilled over the confines of a book about wartime adventures ... When I was freed by my chief or when I freed him from von Zoyton's clutches—which, to my joy, happened several times—I would close my eyes, let my uninhabited imagination take me where it wanted, King's thanks quickly changed into passionate and precise movements, I would turn onto my side and ejaculate into my underwear. This was bliss! I was finally past the time when the Judaeo-Christianity of my early childhood overwhelmed me with guilt after masturbating; now I assumed the act fully, especially when King was the object and Troublay the alibi ...

None of the "Signe de Piste" books, though they're well-known, particularly because of their tendentious illustrations, as homoerotic in content, ever transported me sexually as much as Captain Johns' books that told the adventures of King's Kittens.

I've kept a special place for Trapper Troublay in my teenage reading memories, especially because my separation from him was so abrupt, even violent.

A second surprise, after my encounter with Madame Pilozzi at Household Finance, was waiting for me that August afternoon, a rather intense shock in fact, and if I'd had any idea about what was brewing, I'd have let my mother finish the book instead of taking it back. One of the great amorous adventures of my life was about to end in disappointment and rancour. For the first and only time in my existence, I was furious with someone who wrote novels.

I returned to the chapter I'd abandoned earlier, glad to be back with King and his three assistants—Copper Collson, Nigel Peters, *aka* Cub, and my favourite, Trapper Troublay. Everything was going smoothly, someone, Troublay most likely, was being held prisoner, von Zoyton proved to be more sadistic than ever, King turned up in his faded pilot's uniform, gun at the ready and, in my fertile imagination, soaked in sweat ... He may have smelled a little strong, but it was the smell of deliverance ... and of indescribable joys to come.

It was going to be a fabulous afternoon.

But then a word came along and punched me between the eyes. Everything came to a halt, my left hand stopped fiddling with the red leatherette, my foot stopped beating its own rhythm because of my terrible agitation, my mind stopped working, my heart stopped pounding ...

Just as King was stepping into the room to free Trapper Troublay, there was a reference to his moustache.

His *moustache!*

King had never worn a moustache! Incredulous, I reread the sentence several times, incredulous but there it was, spelled out clearly: King was well and truly a man with a moustache.

I set the book down again.

For months I'd been in love with someone and I didn't know he sported a moustache. I forced myself not to run straight to the library to leaf through all the books about King that I'd read, in search of that stupid moustache on the captain of King's Kittens. But I was positive, *absolutely positive*, that my favourite hero had never worn one! Captain Johns couldn't do that to me! I picked up the book again, reread the passage one more time, tried to imagine my very own King with a black line under his nose ...

No! It could not be!

Betrayal!

I flung the book against the bedroom door. It spun around, making a sound like wings, and crashed to the floor like a bird that had been shot.

I crossed my arms, folded my legs, sank into the La-Z-Boy with a hole in my belly and my heart a wreck.

It was not so much the loss of King himself that was putting me in that state, I don't think—after all, he'd never been anything but the object of my overflowing sexual energy—it was knowing that from now on, my huge need for physical release didn't have an object.

With King gone from my life, whom was I going to be attracted to now? Was I condemned to stay all by myself in my double room on the Plateau Mont-Royal, sprawled in my mother's chair trying to find a fictional hero worthy of my affection? I saw myself skimming novels, begging for a hero to admire, to love, and the ridiculousness of the situation made me burst into dramatic sobs. Whom was I going to be able to love? Love isn't something you can order!

The red leatherette was soaked with tears and slobber, my wet T-shirt sleeve was sticking to my skin, and I had to pee, but I didn't dare to leave the room in case I ran into Mama.

I wiped my eyes, pulled myself out of the La-Z-Boy as best I could, picked up the book, opened it again to the page where King, who'd come to free Trapper Troublay from the clutches of the odious von Zoyton ... What if I tried to forget those few words that had just burst my balloon, acted as if they'd never been thought, written, printed?

No dice. What I'd read, I'd read, and I couldn't change it. After all, you can't ask the hero of an adventure novel to shave off his moustache.

So I turned against the author.

Lousy writer! Moron! To write all those books about the same hero and never mention his moustache! To demolish with just a few words his readers' image of his hero at the very beginning of his adventures! What a jerk! Did he never re-read what he'd written? Did he not make a plan, work on his structure, didn't he keep detailed descriptions of the recurring characters, who would therefore always look the same, have the same physical and psychological traits? Did he not care about his readers—or did he just write to earn a living? To make money?

I stroked the book gently. My pain was really very great, I'd spent such wonderful moments over the English Channel or North Africa, dropping bombs on the German army or chasing planes lighter and more sophisticated than mine, destroying every one because of my tremendous intelligence and my steadfast physical and mental state ... Not to mention the hours I'd spent in the arms of the captain of King's Kittens. I had been my leader's favourite kitty, how would I be able to survive now?

I wasn't at all sure that I could do without Captain W.E. Johns altogether, so for the time being I decided to eliminate only the books about King, and to concentrate on Biggles and Worrals who were unlikely to let me down.

***

"Did you finish it?"

"I guess so."

"Was it good?"

"I guess so."

"Good grief, is that all you can say? You usually go on and on about what you're reading ... "

"I guess so."

"Michel, I'm talking to you!"

"I know that!"

"If you don't change your tone of voice you'll get a slap!"

"I don't want to tell you how it ends, that's all."

"Is it a good ending?"

I give my mother a long look. I hope she won't see my tear-stained cheeks and my sopping wet shirt. But as I've mentioned before, she always sees everything.

"You know, I'm not really sure if it's good or not ... "

PATIRA

Raoul de Navery

"Finished already?"

"It doesn't take forever to read books like those, Mama ... "

"But you had three."

"It just took one day each."

"And was it good?"

"I guess ... "

"You don't sound very sure."

"Umm, yes, it was good. Really good, but ... "

"But what? It was really good, period! I loved it! And I don't want you criticizing those books to me, understand?"

"I didn't criticize, Mama, I didn't say a thing!"

"Not yet, maybe, but I know what's coming!"

"Mama! I told you, I thought it was really good! But there're some things I didn't understand ... "

"I see ... If that's all it is ... What was it you didn't understand? It wasn't all that complicated."

"It's easy to follow the story, but ... How come there are so many abandoned children in French novels?"

"Why are you asking me that? Are there a lot?"

"I think so ... In *L'Auberge de l'Ange-Gardien* the two children are abandoned, in *Sans Famille*, little Rémi is abandoned, they often are in fairytales ... And now in *Patira* ... "

"Poor little Patira, don't you feel sorry for him?"

"Sure I feel sorry for him, but ... do people in France abandon their children just like that? If you read their books you'd think that all the roads of France are full of abandoned children who're starving to death and filthy as pigs!"

"They're just books, Michel."

"I know that, but I still think it happens pretty often ... "

"Those books are set in the past ... Maybe back then, I don't know, maybe in France they used to abandon their children because they couldn't provide for them ... "

"Oh sure, but there's poor people here too and you don't find abandoned children on every corner! They don't abandon children here, for pete's sake! They'd never get away with it! Didn't those people in France get arrested?"

"Look, there are books where mothers leave their newborn babies on the church steps ... Those people can't get caught. You can't ask a newborn baby to remember who its father and mother were! Especially if it's an unwed mother who dropped him off right after he was born ... "

"I don't understand how you can stick up for them."

"I'm not sticking up for them, I think it's just as horrible as you do, but what do you want me to say? I'm trying to find an explanation! You asked me a question and I'm trying to answer it! Maybe there are abandoned children in novels because it's an interesting way to start a story! People want to know where they've come from, why their parents didn't want them ... Like little Patira, when he's abandoned by the travelling acrobats who'd brought him up without knowing where he came from, and now you want to know? Do you think I do?"

"Even if you were poor, you'd never leave me on the steps of a church."

"I've been poor, buster, believe me!"

"See ... "

"Maybe I just wasn't brave enough!"

"Mama!"

"Come on, Michel, I was kidding! I'd never have abandoned you, I wanted you so badly! Mind you, if I'd known ... "

"Aren't you funny!"

"Anyway, here and France aren't the same thing."

"That's what I wanted to know."

"Don't put words in my mouth!"

"You just said in France it isn't like here!"

"I didn't mean that the French are always abandoning their children on the steps of their churches, and don't you dare say that I did, I know you, you'll blab it all over and people will think I'm a cold fish! Maybe the French just do that in their books!"

"Aren't books supposed to be like what really happens?"

"You're trying my patience, Michel ... "

"No I'm not, I'm just asking you a question!"

"What am I supposed to answer? I'm not a literature specialist! I just read books, I follow the story, I cry when it's sad and I laugh when it's funny ... I don't ask myself questions that go on forever at the end of every sentence! I'd never get through a book if I did! I know if I like a story or not and I read the book and that's that! I don't give a hoot if the French abandon their children or not if Patira's story gives me a good cry! And I cried so much when I read *Patira*, I thought I'd cried away ten pounds of tears by the end, and that made me very happy!"

"You always cry when you read."

"I like sad books."

"You sure got your money's worth with that one!"

"I'll say! When that poor Blanche de Couette-Couenne ... "

"Coëtquen, Mama."

"That's what I said."

"You said Couette-Couenne ... "

"That's how I got used to saying it, it was easier to remember. Anyway, when poor Blanche gave birth to her baby in the castle dungeon because her two rotten brothers-in-law had locked her up there six months before and then Patira turned up with his little file to file through the bars because Blanche put her baby out the cellar window and Patira put the baby onto some reeds tied together that made this kind of raft ... "

"That part of the story doesn't make sense, Mama ... "

"What do you mean, doesn't make sense?"

"You know, locking up a poor pregnant woman in the dungeon in the middle of winter ... "

"There's no season for rotten men, Michel! They were jealous of her because people said she'd usurped her title of Marquise and they wanted to get rid of her at any price. They were prepared to do anything and they did it!"

"Mama! Blanche de Coëtquen spends *the whole winter* in the dungeon that was so damp there was water running down the walls, she sleeps on a straw mat spread out on a wooden ledge, all she has to eat is black bread and water, there are floods in the spring, she's in cold water up to her chin, she hasn't got a change of clothes, she hasn't got any light, she gives birth to her baby lying on her wooden ledge with no doctor to help her, the bars of her prison get filed away with this thing the size of a nail-file, she scrapes her hands, she bleeds, she hasn't even got any mercurochrome to put on her cuts—*and it doesn't kill her!*"

"What do you mean doesn't kill her! She dies at the end of the first book and it's so sad I thought I'd never get over it!"

"But before she dies she's set free by this sleepwalker, she finds her baby *dangling* over a fire that's burning the both of them, him and that crazy Jeanne that was looking after him and didn't know who he was, she's saved for the second time by Patira ... And she dies a beautiful death, kissing her child and then blessing everybody! Really!"

"If that death didn't make you cry, young man, you haven't got a heart!"

"I guess I haven't got a heart then!"

"Michel! When she realizes just before she dies that her hair went white while she was locked away even though she's just *eighteen years old*, I thought I was going to die too ... don't tell me that didn't have any effect on you!"

"I thought it didn't make any sense. Eighteen years old with white hair—come off it!"

"Even if it didn't make sense, it was still sad."

"See, you just said it yourself—it didn't make sense!"

"It wouldn't've made any sense in real life, Michel, but it did in the book! And that's what counts! All the malarkey you read in those books of yours about the adventures of Biggles and in Jules Verne's novels and Tintin and your Scarlet Pimpernel, d'you think they'd make any sense in real life? Well, do you? No! But you still believe them!"

"Jules Verne's books are based on science, you know! Patira isn't! For pete's sake, she's locked up *inside* the castle, a castle isn't the size of Montreal, you know, but nobody hears her yelling!"

"She's at the far end of the castle, the far end of the property, the far end of the moat—*in the dungeon*, it's explained very clearly, so don't argue with me!"

"And there's never even one person walking around nearby?"

"Of course not! There's all kinds of puddles and mud and frogs and bugs ... "

"Come on! She'd just have to yell for help a little louder and everybody'd hear her!"

"People hear her when she yells, but they think it's a ghost. Can't you read? They think she's the ghost of that Couette-Couenne woman! There's a song about it in the book! You must've skipped some parts when you read it!"

"I did not!"

"So when they hear her moaning they're scared to death!"

"They're all pretty stupid, the whole bunch of them!"

"Enough arguing. I'm going to lose my temper!"

"And besides, she never goes to the toilet!"

"What do you mean, she never goes to the toilet?"

"Simon, her jailer, brings her a jug of water every day, don't tell me she pees in it! And where does she do number two?"

"Michel, for heaven's sake! They aren't going to tell us where people do number two in books!"

"Didn't you ever wonder where she did it, in the dungeon?"

"Of course not! And I don't *want* to know!"

"Well I do!"

"In those books of Jules Verne's, do they tell you?"

"Hardly, but if they're lost in a forest in the Amazon, you can always guess. But we're talking about *her*, Mama! She spends the whole winter in a damp dungeon! I can't believe she was constipated for six months! And if she isn't constipated and she does it in the corner of her cell, it would stink to high heaven after a few weeks, unless Simon cleans it up ... "

"Michel! I won't allow you to make fun of one of my favourite books!"

"I'm not making fun of it, Mama! I just want to know something, that's all!"

"Well I don't! First of all, it never crossed my mind that Blanche de Couette-Couenne even does it ... And how's the author supposed to tell us? 'She crouched in a corner and did her business and then Simon arrived with a shovel and cleaned it up.' It's a novel, Michel, we don't need to know things like that! When you read *The Count of Monte Cristo* last year, did Alexandre Dumas tell you where Edmond Dantès did number two?"

"No, you're right ... "

"See, you didn't even wonder! But now you're showing bad faith just because it's *Patira* and I like it!"

"I'm not showing bad faith, Mama, it's just that's the first time I've ever wondered ... Anyway, the whole business with the jealous brothers-in-law, I don't believe it. I mean really!"

"Why not?"

"They never accepted her because she wasn't a real princess, and if she wasn't a real princess then she doesn't deserve to be part of their family: do you believe that?"

"Sure I do!"

"What's a real princess anyway?"

"What do you mean, what's a real princess?"

"I mean ... what is it that makes a princess a real princess?"

"Well, she's the daughter of a prince and a princess, that's what! You know as well as I do!"

"And what about the others, her parents, how did they know they were a prince and a princess?"

"It's the same thing, they had noble parents!"

"What does that mean, they had noble parents?"

"Michel, you read French novels all year long, you must know what nobles are, don't ask me to tell you! They're people with blue blood!"

"Blue blood?"

"That's right!"

"When they cut themselves it comes out blue?"

"Hardly! That's just a way of talking! It's an expression; their blood isn't really blue ... it's noble blood!

"I don't understand."

"Now listen. I'm not an expert on the history of France, it was the history of Canada they taught us when I was a little girl in Saskatchewan ... "

"Here too—and I'm sick and tired of hearing about Louis Hébert and Marie Rollet!"

"Well apparently ... When the first king of France arrived ... "

"How'd they know he was the king of France?"

"Keep quiet and listen. It was a Louis if I remember right. They all were, all the kings of France were Louis ... It must've been Louis One. Or Louis the First. Anyway, the good Lord appeared to him ... "

"The good Lord appeared to him?"

"Apparently."

"But usually he doesn't appear himself, he sends some-body else—the Blessed Virgin or some angels ... "

"I know, but this time was special, it was for the king of France! And quit interrupting me! So anyway, he told him he'd been picked to be the king of France and starting right then and there, to make sure people would know who they were, him and his descendants would have blue blood!"

"But you just told me it wasn't really blue!"

"I'm trying to explain, it's an expression!"

"Okay, okay, but how do they know they've got blue blood if it isn't blue?"

"They know because it gets passed on! From father to son! Like ... like a name! Your name is Tremblay because your father's a Tremblay! And if your father had blue blood, you'd have blue blood too! Now do you understand?"

"So you mean that Blanche de Coëtquen, when she was still Blanche Halgan, she didn't have blue blood because her father was a ship's captain and not a king ... "

"That's right. And since it's seen as a bad thing for nobles to marry somebody who isn't noble, Tanguy Couette-Couenne's two brothers don't like it when he marries the daughter of a ship's captain instead of a girl that's more important!"

"And then when she marries him her blood turns blue?"

"What're you talking about! You don't get blue blood from your husband, you get it from your father!"

"What about their children? Would their blood be half-and-half? That whole business sounds really stupid ... "

"It's not stupid, Michel, it comes from the good Lord."

"Listen! If I said that the good Lord appeared to me and told me he was crowning me the king of Canada, would my blood turn blue?"

"Hardly. If you said that nobody'd believe you!"

"I know that. So how come they believed him?"

"Because with him it was true!"

"It could be true for me too!"

"I'm your mother, Michel, and I'd know it wasn't true."

"He must've had a mother too! She'd've believed him but you wouldn't believe me!"

"Maybe he saved his country from bandits and thieves but you didn't save anybody from anything!"

"Just you wait!"

"Michel, quit pulling my leg."

"Oh sure, and you believe everything they say in books!"

"I'll tell you, it's a lot more interesting than arguing with you! You've been asking questions ever since you were born, till we ran out of ways to make things up."

"Ha ha! You just admitted it, you make things up!"

"If I took all the answers I've made up since you were born and laid them end to end, I might be a great novelist today! And rich! And let me tell you, we wouldn't be cooped up here on Cartier Street across from the Mont-Royal Convent!"

"That reminds me. Those girls that go to the convent, Mama, they're rich, aren't they?"

"You said it! Just look at the cars they come back in on Sunday night."

"Have they got blue blood?"

"No! Nobody in America's got blue blood, Michel, it's just in Europe."

"How come?"

"How should I know ... Maybe because they've been around longer than we have ... If we'd been there before, maybe the rest of us would have blue blood too! I guess we just aren't old enough ... "

"But your grandparents were Cree ... "

"That's right."

"And they'd been here for a long, long time before the Europeans came ... "

"True."

"So first of all, how come the good Lord never appeared to tell them they had blue blood? Did he just appear in Europe? If you ask me, that's unfair! There ought to be one Cree somewhere that deserves to be a noble who's crowned the king of the Cree like those people over there!"

"That's true, you know, it isn't fair. You're absolutely right. But what can I tell you, it comes from the good Lord ... and the Cree don't know the good Lord."

"It was them, the Europeans, that said it comes from the good Lord! We don't have to believe them Did the good Lord come and tell you it was true, that he'd appeared to every first king of every country in Europe and told him his blood was blue?"

"Sure, but it happened so long ago there must be proof of it by now."

"We never saw any of that proof!"

"Are you trying to tell me that the first one, that Louis One, made it all up so he'd get to be king of France, and that everybody that believed him was stupid? Right up till the French Revolution?"

"I don't know ... "

"That all those Louis, from the first till the ... How many were there anyway? Anyway, that the whole bunch of them were liars? You're a real doubting Thomas! Anyway, there haven't been any kings in France ever since they had that revolution. And that settles it."

"But they've got nobles."

"As far as that's concerned ... "

"And all kinds of bluebloods ... "

"Not all kinds, just some."

"And they've got a queen in Belgium. And a beautiful new one in England."

"That's right, my beautiful Princess Elizabeth that I love so much is a queen now! So young! And there's her sister, Princess Margaret Rose, now that's a little beauty! Don't say one thing against them, I love them so much! Even though they've got blue blood, they haven't got a snobbish bone in their bodies, neither one! Let me tell you, those two deserve to be noble!"

"Don't try changing the subject, Mama, I know you love the English royal family, you always talk as if you see them every day! But what I want to know is, did the good Lord appear to the first king of England too?"

"He must have."

"And he said the same things he said to the French one?"

"I suppose so."

"In English?"

"If he talked French to the other one he must've talked English to that one ... "

"And then his blood turned blue!"

"That's enough about blue blood, it's like you were talking about a disease! And it isn't a disease, Michel, it's a gift from heaven, a blessing! If the good Lord gave it to them it had to be because they deserved it! In English or French! And in Spanish for the king of Spain! And Italian for the king of Italy! I wonder though, have they got a king in Italy?"

"You really believe all that?"

"Well, you know, I'm starting to wonder ... I'd never thought about it that way before ... And some Cree must've deserved it too ... "

"So if we go back to the first king of France, being a noble is something you earn, is that it?"

"That's it."

"So you mean Blanche de Coëtquen earned the right to have blue blood when she got married to Tanguy even though she wasn't born with it like him ... "

"That's right."

"And then her two brothers-in-law, Florent and Gaël, were really rotten and didn't deserve to live because they were so cruel to their poor sister-in-law!"

"That's right."

"Blue blood or no ... "

"That's right, and I'll have you know I was glad when they paid for their crimes! I kissed the book, I hugged it ... "

"So maybe the French Revolution was a good thing after all."

"Sure it was good, I never said it wasn't! The poor people were starving to death while the nobles were stuffing their faces! Marie-Antoinette was gobbling Viennese pastries while the people were crying like the damned at the gates of Versailles with their shovels and their scythes. We saw all that in the movie with Norma Shearer. But what's this about the French Revolution all of a sudden? It hasn't got anything to do with that book!"

"Because Raoul de Navery says the opposite in *Le Trésor de l'abbaye*, the book that comes after *Patira* ... You're the one that skipped some parts. He describes the revolutionaries as bloodthirsty monsters, all hunchbacked and ugly and deformed and one-eyed and limping and they stink and they kill the poor bluebloods ... The only thing they want is to take their place."

"Michel, don't start again! We've discussed this enough, we aren't going to settle the question of the French Revolution in one afternoon! When I start a discussion with you I never know where it's going to end! And by the way, quit saying *moé* and *toé*, you know I hate that! I taught you how to speak properly, so speak properly! And next time I read a good book I'm not telling you! I'll keep it to myself, that way I'll be sure I can go on liking it!"

BONHEUR D'OCCASION (The Tin Flute)

Gabrielle Roy

Great excitement in the house. We—my mother, my father, Jacques, and me—were going to drive around the Gaspé Peninsula. A week-long trip prepared in minute detail by my brother, who had concocted a detailed itinerary so that we wouldn't waste any time: the first night, we'd sleep in Quebec City, the second in Sainte-Luce-sur-mer, the third in Paspébiac, the fourth in Percé and so on.

I had just turned fourteen, I was covered with pimples, I was so nervous I drove everybody crazy (Mama: "If you don't quit squirming you'll be having an operation on your glands!"), I spent my days buried under a pile of books, avoiding the sun and, almost, the daylight; and of course I was the only one who didn't feel like going on the trip.

"The fresh air will be good for you!"

"I heard that it smells like the devil!"

"It doesn't smell like the devil, it smells like dried fish!"

"That's just as bad!"

"Maybe so, but it's good for you anyway! Maybe it cures the awkward age! And I warn you, you aren't spending two hours in the toilet like you do at home in the motels where we sleep! You'll do your ... your reading by the seaside—that will be romantic and you won't be so pale!"

We were supposed to go by way of Quebec City, detour through Charlevoix County, the Quebec cradle of the

Tremblays, then take the ferry to the Gaspé, but I didn't care about any of it. I had adored my Grandmother Tremblay, but I couldn't see the point of travelling hundreds of miles to see the house where she was born. Just the site, actually, because the house had been gone for ages.

"Apparently the boats leaving from La Malbaie is a gorgeous sight."

"We can see that from here, they come to Montreal!"

"See here, how would you like a whack on the head?"

But little by little, Mama's excitement became infectious—she'd turned ten years younger on the night in June when the decision was made to take the trip—and I started champing at the bit in silence so I wouldn't spoil her fun.

My friends thought I was lucky ("The Gaspé! You'll find all kinds of agates by the seaside!"), I thought they were jerks.

On the morning of our departure, suitcases were strewn along the floor in the hallway; Monsieur Migneault, our roomer, had got up early to help us take them down to the sidewalk, but we'd have preferred it if he'd stayed in bed: even at seven a.m. he reeked of perfume. Worse, in fact: he smelled of perfume from the night before!

Mama had had a toothache during the night and we'd been afraid that we wouldn't be able to go—which would have suited me fine—but a few drops of oil of cloves had taken care of it and we piled into my brother's powder blue Chevrolet in a state of near-hysteria. My father had never learned how to drive because of his deafness, so Jacques would be the only driver for the whole trip.

As for me, finally I did have a reason for wanting to go to the Gaspé. Mama had just given me a magnificent gift.

Just before we left, she'd taken me aside.

"What are you taking to read?"

"I wanted to re-read the Prince Érics in the 'Signe de Piste.' I know them by heart but they're so wonderful!"

"Never mind that. I've got something for you ... After *Patira*, I swore that never again would I read the same book as you, but this ... "

She was holding against her two limp, dog-eared volumes, books that had been read many times, with passion.

"Read this. Your cousin Jeannine lent it to me ... It's amazing. What it did to me ... I can't tell you what it did to me .... Mind you, though, I don't want any arguments like the one we had after *Patira!* Say just one word against this book and I won't feed you for the rest of the summer!"

Gabrielle Roy's *Bonheur d'occasion*. I'd seen it lying around the house for a week now, I'd heard Mama sing its praises with tears in her voice; she talked about a family called Lacasse, in Saint-Henri, a neighbourhood far from ours, which I didn't know at all, she talked about conscription—my father had explained what that meant—about the unjust death of a child in a hospital because his parents were too poor to get proper treatment for him, and about a house so close to the railway tracks that everything in the Lacasse apartment shook whenever a train went by. She talked about a tremendous love story interrupted by the war and by the cowardice of the young man, Jean Lévesque, who took off after seducing the heroine, Florentine Lacasse, who went on loving him anyway, the lunatic; about an unhappy marriage so that Jean Lévesque's child would have a father; about the departure for the war of three men from the same family—father, son and son-in-law—on board the same train that was probably taking them to their death ("Now everybody knows it, our men served as cannon fodder during the Normandy landing!"); about the daily misery of French-Canadians during the war finally being described in a great novel, a novel as great and wonderful as the great French novels our family loved so much.

"It's absolutely fantastic. You know that Gabrielle Roy won a prize in France for this book a few years ago? The Prix

Fémina. It's not as important as the Prix Goncourt apparently, but it's still really important."

She had offered it to me like some precious and delicate object that you can't place in the hands of just anyone.

"It may be a little serious for you, but I think you can read it anyway ... You're still a little brat, but you're old for your age ... "

"Can I bring it along to the Gaspé?"

"That's why I'm lending it to you. I know you aren't too crazy about going on this trip ... But if you read this book I promise you, the week's going to pass quickly!"

"You'll let me read it whenever I want though ... "

"What do you mean?"

"I mean, if I feel like reading in the car ... "

"Won't you get carsick?"

"I'll try and we'll see ... "

"Mind you, I don't want you throwing up out of pig-headedness!"

"Don't worry ... And if I want to read in the motels, let me!"

"At least you'll take a look at the places we visit now and then; don't scare me!"

"Okay, but I don't want you yelling at me if I like it so much that I want to read without stopping ... "

"Watch it, Michel ... "

"Mama, don't start!"

"It's true, last week I nearly burned two meals, I was so deep in that book ... "

"See ... "

"But when we say something to you I want an answer! I can't stand it when you don't answer."

***

Needless to say I saw nothing in the Gaspé, or almost nothing. Of the trip there I have a vague memory of Quebec City, which I'd never seen and thought was very pretty in the July sunlight; I see my mother sitting in a lawn chair on the terrace of the Manoir Richelieu at La Malbaie, saying with a gorgeous smile: "We haven't been here since our honeymoon, Armand—thirty years ago!" while my father hid his emotion by pretending to cough into his fist; I also got a glimpse of a big white ship and Papa, with his arm raised, saying: "My father and mother left here on a boat like that one ... If they hadn't come to Montreal, Nana, we'd never have met!" As for the ferry, the one that I picture now looks like those that go between Quebec City and Lévis. Had we come back to the capital to cross the St. Lawrence? Probably, because I have no memory of Tadoussac or the mouth of the Saguenay.

Of the old road along the south shore that circles the Gaspé Peninsula, the one people avoid nowadays because they're in such a hurry but that's so beautiful, so impressive with its fjords and its hills crumbling into the sea— Rimouski, Kamouraska, Saint-Pacôme, Cacouna, Rivière-du-Loup—all I can see, if I take my eyes off *Bonheur d'occasion*, is my two feet resting between the front seats, the profile of my brother, concentrating on the road ahead of him, and behind us, a patch of flawlessly blue sky.

And I hear Mama saying: "Michel, we're at Le Bic, one of the most beautiful places in the Province of Quebec, and you've still got your nose in your book! If you don't sit up this minute you'll be getting a Chinese whack and you'll be starched for the rest of the trip!"

I'd brought that expression home from school a few months earlier; she'd thought it was very funny and was always repeating it, wiping her eyes from laughing so much, but for a few weeks now she'd been using it on me a lot and I was afraid that she'd carry out her threat. My mother's whacks were very rare, but they were Chinese, and they left you stiff and starched, all right!

Curled up in the foetal position, lying on my back with my head against my father's leg or my mother's, depending on the day, feet sticking out the window or resting on the blazing-hot floor of the car, devouring a Lowney's chocolate bar or chewing a stick of Thrills gum, I was reading Gabrielle Roy, indifferent to the beauty of the landscapes all around us, unmoved by the men's protests and my mother's increasingly detailed threats.

"If you don't put that book down I'll make you eat it!"

"You're the one that lent it to me!"

"Don't make me wish that I hadn't! I told you not to read in the car too much!"

"I can't stop, it's too good!"

"For heaven's sake! It isn't chocolate cake!"

"It's better."

"Now you listen to me! Give me that book, give it to me this minute! There's a limit! GIVE IT TO ME OR I'LL COME AND GET IT MYSELF!"

Reluctantly I closed it and looked indifferently at the splendours of my country.

"Don't tell me that isn't a gorgeous sight, those two big rocks in the sea! People come from the ends of the earth to see Le Bic, and you're sitting there with your nose in a book! You can't ignore something as beautiful as that, Michel, you haven't got the right!"

"Sure, sure, I know, it's beautiful ... "

"Look at the sea ... it's the first time you've seen it! And smell how good it smells!"

"It isn't even the real sea ... "

"What do you mean, it isn't the real sea?"

"You can still see the other shore, you just showed me."

"Michel, don't put words in my mouth! The water's salty so it's the sea!"

When I was quite sure that she'd stopped watching me I opened my book discreetly and plunged back into the tragedy of the Lacasse family in Saint-Henri, which I intended to visit as soon as I could; my soul was back in Montreal, which I should never have left, my heart was shuddering in unison with that of Florentine, who was waiting for her Jean Lévesque, who'd given herself to her Jean Lévesque, who'd lost her Jean Lévesque, who started again to wait for him ...

"Michel, I can hear you reading!"

At school we were given very few Quebec writers to read and never, but never an entire book. I remember analyzing parts of *Les Anciens Canadiens*, by Philippe-Aubert de Gaspé—19th century Quebec folklore didn't interest me and I was bored to death—excerpts from *Andante, Allegro* or *Adagio* by Félix Leclerc—only to be told, of course, that La Fontaine's *Fables* were infinitely superior; I have a vague memory of reading a description from *Le Survenant*, by Germaine Guèvremont, the part, I think, where the wind lifts the skirts of Angélina Desmarais, only to be told that such matters shouldn't be written about because they could lead to several interpretations; it had to be Catholic and edifying and at fourteen, I was getting impatient, starting to be fed up with pious thoughts—the last thing that my own were!—and edifying examples.

Bonheur d'occasion had none of that, not from the standpoint of religion at any rate. This was the first time I was reading a novel written in my city in which virtue and propriety weren't featured as absolute masters, in which the Catholic religion didn't answer all the questions, in which God was not automatically at the end of every fate, and I was amazed. So chaos existed in Montreal elsewhere than in my soul? And I wasn't alone in my corner, beginning to suspect that we were lied to, that we'd been deceived forever?

There was no moral code in this novel, poverty wasn't explained, cowardice wasn't punished, a pregnant young girl wasn't guilty of an indelible sin, war was not a noble mission to save democracy but a monstrosity that crushed the little people and protected the rich.

In *Bonheur d'occasion* I found answers to questions I was beginning to wonder about, the people in it were like me, they expressed themselves the way I did, they struggled the way my parents did, they suffered injustice without finding a way out, and sometimes they paid with their lives for other people's mistakes.

Mama had talked about cannon fodder. So that was what it meant! Workers like my father who went to war not to save France or England from the clutches of the wicked Nazis—we were a long way from King and Biggles—but to support their families because they couldn't find work back home and who got sent away to be massacred in the front lines because they weren't educated.

So *Bonheur d'occasion* was an *atheistic* novel like some of those French ones that my mother practically went into hiding to read ("You aren't old enough!") and that my Grandmother Tremblay had read before her! And why had she given me this one to read?

I looked more closely, I studied the lengthy descriptions of the characters' states of mind: Rose-Anna Lacasse, who gave birth to a baby on the day of her daughter's wedding while suffering over the imminent loss of her eight-year-old, Daniel, who was slowly dying of leukemia; Florentine, who was marrying Emmanuel Létourneau without telling him that she could never love him and that she was pregnant by Jean Lévesque; Azarius Lacasse, who was joining the army at thirty-nine to feed his family, and I thought: "That's life, that's what life is really like, there aren't any explanations for injustice—and no solution either! The good Lord isn't going to appear like Superman to save them all, those characters are lost!" And all that, the great tragic lives of some little people, was taking place not in far-off nineteenth-century Paris during the tremendous changes made by Haussmann, or in the trenches of Berezina during the Napoleonic wars, but here where I lived, in my own language, my own sensibility, my own understanding of my own world, insignificant though it may be.

I was more than overwhelmed by the grandeur of the writing and the author's dramatic sense, I was awed and grateful that such a powerful story had been written in my country, my province, my city!

So it was possible!

***

At Sainte-Flavie, where we were supposed to turn right to go inland and drive through the mountains that led to the Baie des Chaleurs, my brother changed his mind and continued straight ahead. My father noticed right away, and thinking Jacques had made a mistake, pointed it out to him.

I was reading next to Papa, with my legs folded under me. My brother looked at me in the rear-view mirror.

"Tell him I changed my mind, we'll see the Baie des Chaleurs on the way back."

I was halfway through the second volume, Emmanuel Létourneau was looking all over Saint-Henri for Florentine so he could ask her to marry him, and I replied with a vague growl that infuriated Jacques.

"Michel, I'm talking to you! I haven't asked you for anything since we left, but now I want you to explain to Papa."

"All right, all right, I heard, I'm not deaf!"

Meanwhile my father, who didn't know what we were talking about, continued to wave his arms, telling Jacques that he'd made a mistake, he should have turned right ... and then, to put the icing on the cake, my mother decided to get involved. With difficulty she turned around, reached out, and tapped Papa's hand.

"He knows that, Armand!"

"What?"

"He knows!"

"He knows what? That he made a mistake? Why not just make a U-turn?"

"He didn't make a mistake!"

"What d'you mean he didn't make a mistake? He should've turned right at Saint-Flavie, it's right there on the map, in big letters! Look!"

"Turn up your hearing aid, then you'll be able to hear what we're saying."

"I can't, it's up as high as it'll go!"

My mother turned towards me, furious.

"You explain it to him, for the love of God, you selfish brat! I'm sure people can hear us shouting all the way to the Gaspé! All I want is thirty seconds of your precious time! You're sitting beside him, he can read your lips. And give me that book, I don't know why I lent it to you, you're ruining your eyes! A deaf man and a blind boy in one family is too much!"

She grabbed the book and shoved it into the glove compartment.

"Sometimes I envy mothers with children who can't read."

I knew that was false, she was using bad faith, as usual, to get her own way, and I turned to Papa who was still shouting that no one ever listened to him, that we all took him for an idiot, but that we'd soon realize that he was right, as usual.

He listened to my explanations and shrugged.

"What're you talking about? He just said that because he made a mistake and he won't turn around because he's too proud!"

Now my brother shrugged.

We continued in silence for a few minutes. My father, obviously furious, couldn't contain himself for very long.

"My mother always said, you shouldn't go around the Gaspé Peninsula clockwise! Because it's more beautiful the other way. Because you see more. But Mister Know-It-All knows better than her!"

The atmosphere was poisonous and I didn't dare ask for my book. For once, I had my head up to look at the scenery and Mama wasn't in awe, she was acting as if there was nothing worth looking at.

But the beauty of the sea, the play of light on the waves, the cool breeze from the open water finally calmed us a little. We were still silent, but the hostility was melting in the splendour of the morning.

When we arrived at Percé, after eating a rather chewy roast chicken in Gaspé because none of us liked fish (Mama: "That's just like us, coming to the Gaspé to eat chicken!"), a thick, creamy fog covered everything and we couldn't see the sky or the sea or the famous rock, and though the village was small, we spent a long time looking for the Trois Soeurs motel where we were to spend the night.

Mama was exasperated.

"Driving five hundred miles to end up in a fog bank, honestly!"

My brother tried to console her.

"Sometimes there's fog in the morning but then it lifts and it's fine for the rest of the day ... "

"Sometimes?"

I of course was only thinking about *Bonheur d'occasion*. I was trying to think up with some way to get my hands on the book without Mama realizing, but the four of us were always together so I couldn't go into hiding and read it.

The fog was taking a long time to lift and I could see with horror the moment coming when one of the other three would get up to announce that we were going back to Montreal. They were all quite capable of doing that and the threat hovered over us well into the afternoon.

Around three o'clock we were outside the little theatre in Percé, which had just opened, (Denise Pelletier, Guy Provost and Georges Groulx were doing Pirandello's *The Man With the Flower in His Mouth*, I think), when all at once, with no help from the wind, only through the power of the sun, the fog lifted and the Percé rock appeared, so close to the shore that at first we thought it was a huge boat moored there, and so beautiful that Mama burst into tears.

I was very impressed by that gigantic block of stone lying motionless by the seaside, but I knew that the time had come to speak to Mama. I'd have to take advantage of her tears and the fact that her heart was melting before such beauty to remind her that she had no right to stop me from finishing Gabrielle Roy's novel.

She cut me off after a few words.

"Don't spoil my fun! When you've seen everything there is to see in Percé—the rock, Bonaventure Island, the dried fish, the tide coming in and the cold water, you'll get your book back. And not before!"

And so I finished *Bonheur d'occasion* in the bathroom the next night, sometimes sitting on the rim of the toilet, sometimes lying in the tub. The end overwhelmed me more than all the rest. The three men from one family going off to war for the wrong reasons; Florentine, a new, unhappy bride, catching sight of her Jean Lévesque, the dirty dog, on the other side of the street, deciding once and for all to stop running after him; Rose-Anna giving birth to a poor little victim whose fate would be no different from that of the other members of his family; the heavy blackness of a working-class tragedy raised to the heights of the great European ones thanks to the huge talent of Gabrielle Roy, all of that, the misery on one side, the talent to recount it on the other, stirred me to the depths of my soul, and I spent part of the night in tears. Over the fate of the Lacasse family, of course. But for the first time in my life, over our collective fate, that of a small people, already lost, abandoned and forgotten amid widespread indifference, drowned in the great History of others, who only remembered us when they needed cannon fodder.

At dawn, Mama came into the bathroom and gave a muffled cry when she saw me.

"What're you doing there? Are you sick?"

I shook my head, showed her the book.

She in turn sat on the toilet seat.

"You finished?"

I nodded.

"Good, isn't it?"

I couldn't speak.

"I knew you'd like it. I let you read it ... "

She looked at me, smiling sadly.

"I don't know ... I figured that you'd understand what was in it ... That you'd understand more than the others what was in it ... You see, it's not often that somebody talks like that about us, about us women ... You, you listen ... Sometimes I think that Gabrielle Roy must've listened like you do a little, when she was a child ... And, well, I'm sorry about this afternoon ... I wasn't thinking ... I don't envy women whose children don't read, on the contrary, I pity them from the bottom of my heart!"

Confidences, *real* confidences wouldn't come, I could sense it, the time wasn't right and the place was too ridiculous. I merely looked at my mother and smiled back.

I closed the book again and got out of the tub, stretching.

"Remember this, Michel, Gabrielle Roy is a genius."

"Yes. Gabrielle Roy is a genius."

"Try not to go to bed right away, the sun will be up soon and they say it's just gorgeous to watch it come up here at Percé, above the sea ... "

But I didn't see the sun rise over the Percé rock that morning; I was sound asleep, hugging the two volumes of *Bonheur d'occasion*. I had found the first idol of my life who was from my own country, and no landscape, not even the most grandiose in the world, could rival my sense of well-being.

AGAMEMNON

Aeschylus

It was a small, rectangular, brown cardboard package tied with string. Mama had found it in the morning mail and she'd put it on the brand-new metal-rimmed grey arborite table that she was so proud of. It was the first time a package had come to our house from Europe and we were very impressed.

When I came home from school, I saw my mother, her brow furrowed, lost in admiration over the small blue stamp. She seemed to doubt that it had really come from France and kept rubbing it with her thumb as if it were an ink-stain on the upper right-hand corner of the package.

"Jacques' book came from France this morning. Just imagine how far it's travelled!"

I had tossed my school bag on the floor and stepped up to the table, practically shaking. At last! It took so long!

"So that's what a parcel from Europe looks like!"

"How come you brought home your school bag?"

"We've got the afternoon off. There's a teachers' meeting."

"Don't tell me you're going to be underfoot for the rest of the day!"

"No I won't, I have to go to the library."

Sitting next to my mother, who had pushed he package towards me, still holding on to it as if she were afraid it would fly away, I stroked it gently. The address was typed onto a strip of white paper:

Jacques Tremblay
4505, rue Cartier
Montréal, P.Q.
CANADA

The string felt rough but the cardboard was rather soft. And it didn't have any smell.

"Why're you putting your nose on it?"

"To see if you can smell the book through the cardboard."

"You like to stick your nose in everything, don't you? I don't know where you picked up that habit. Your father and I don't do that."

She got up from the table, sweeping away some non-existent breadcrumbs.

"You want me to make you some little baloney hats for lunch?"

She'd already planned to make it, I knew that, but she was kind enough to suggest that I had a choice. I adored those greasy, salty, fried baloney slices that took on the shape of little hats oozing grease as they crackled in the pan, that Mama served with cold leftover potatoes, but this time I barely heard her question.

She went to the kitchen. I vaguely heard her take out the huge cast iron frying pan that she always said was going to give her a hernia, set it on the stove and plunk in a lump of butter which immediately started to splutter.

I stood there, not moving, in front of the package that I didn't dare to open because I wasn't sure it really belonged to me. No, I was sure it *did* belong to me but my name wasn't on it, so I hesitated.

A few months earlier my brother Jacques had got a circular from Les Éditions Rencontres in the mail. He'd studied it carefully, left it on his desk to be sure I'd find it and, even more, to make my mouth water. Jacques was now a French teacher in a primary school and he had built himself a magnificent desk of varnished blonde wood—it was the dawning of the age of Varathane—where in fact I'd started writing inconsequential little things, poems, a kind of journal, when he wasn't sitting there to correct assignments. He knew and encouraged my passion for reading even if he often found my choices questionable.

Jacques had explained to me that when you subscribed to Éditions Rencontres, you committed yourself to buy ten books a year (ten books a year, my brother must be rich!) and you got one *free* when you joined.

A *new* book free!

"Apparently the books are gorgeous. Bound in leatherette with imitation gold! And they feel really soft, the covers are padded, the print isn't too small, and every personal library can take pride in owning them. What do you think?"

I'd gone into what my mother called my Saint Vitus's dance, jumping up and down, clapping my hands, shouting like a lunatic, flinging myself into the wine-red monster with the hole in the left armrest that was looking more and more like a crater.

"Control yourself, Michel, you're nearly fifteen years old now, you aren't a child!"

I stood up, put on the mock contrite look I'd been specializing in for a while now and that I thought had everybody fooled.

"You're right ... I'm sorry. It's the excitement ... "

"You'll be sixteen next year, it's about time you dropped those silly books you always read and start on the classics ... "

"Jules Verne's a classic, you know!"

"Jules Verne is ridiculous!"

My brother Jacques had always been quick to judge, implacable and definitive. And I wasn't about to admit that I'd long ago started dipping into his books, that for ages now certain authors on the Index, the ones who were easiest to read—Hugo, Maupassant, Baudelaire—no longer had any secrets from me, or so I thought in my pretentiousness of a teenager who thinks he's smarter than anyone else.

"The book they're offering is three Greek tragedies. I'm not interested so I'll give it to you. When it arrives, you can have it."

I didn't even know what a Greek tragedy was, but I felt like going into my Saint Vitus's dance again.

Throwing my arms around his neck was unthinkable. It wasn't done in our family, not by the men at least. I thanked him as simply as I could—cool on the outside but fiery inside—and at once, started waiting for the package to arrive from France.

Which took its time.

Every noon, when I came home from school, I asked Mama if it had come. She looked up—she hated being interrupted during her favourite radio program, "Jeunesse dorée," every day from noon till twelve-fifteen, which made her wet at least two handkerchiefs per day—shook her head, dove back into the numerous and complicated woes cooked up by the champion of the soaps, Madame Laurette Auger, *aka* Jean Despréz.

"Either open that darn package or don't, but make up your mind!"

A few minutes had passed without my realizing, and I was still admiring the package, which was still intact.

Mama was holding the heavy frying pan and dumping its contents onto a plate at the end of the table. It was not a very pretty sight, those baloney slices, charred in places and covered with a sweat of melted fat, but the penetrating aroma made my mouth water.

I looked up.

Baloney or Aeschylus?

Hard to choose.

I pushed away the book. I didn't want to open the parcel from Les Éditions Rencontres too hastily, I'd waited so long for it and I mustn't spoil the sublime moment when I would remove the volume from its cardboard shell. A book bound in leatherette! With gilt edges! And padded! I who was used to the old tomes from the municipal library.

"You made the right choice. Wait till you've finished eating. And eat it right now, cold baloney's hard to digest, you know!"

"You always say I could digest an iron!"

"Yes, but when you eat too fast the iron starts to steam and then you get sick!"

Once I'd downed the baloney—"Michel, if you see black spots this afternoon, don't come complaining to me!"—washed my hands and carefully wiped my mouth (I suspected that I'd kiss the book before I opened it and I certainly didn't want to leave grease stains), I came back to sit in front of the still-intact package.

The moment had arrived.

I took the chisel from the toolbox under the kitchen sink and headed for my bedroom.

"Michel! Are you sure it's all right for you open that package before your brother comes home?"

"Yes, I told you a hundred times, Jacques gave it to me!"

"He didn't tell me!"

"Mama, don't ruin my day, you can't make me wait till tonight!"

"Okay, go ahead, do what you want, you always do anyway! I'm too good to you! If your brother yells about it afterwards, I'll be the one that picks up the pieces!"

Comfortably ensconced in the La-Z-Boy, I put the package on my knees, cut the string, and wrapped it around my hand to keep as a souvenir. European string! Then I took off the paper, careful not to crumple it or to tear the address and the blue stamp. The paper was brown, rather rough to the touch, and something like the kind we used to cover our schoolbooks, but sturdier. Underneath, some stiff cardboard that opened like a box.

Some papers, a small catalogue, that month's selection, a letter in a typeface that looked like handwriting, and sepia ink that looked really real: "Welcome to our club, Monsieur Tremblay, you have made an excellent selection," and so on.

There it was, sitting in the cardboard like some precious object; it wasn't padded—probably because they were giving it to new subscribers free—but the mock calfskin binding in a fine light brown, nearly caramel, looked elegant. A bouquet of odours—printers' ink, paper, cardboard—rose to my nostrils and I bent over the parcel, closing my eyes.

It's said that desire is more thrilling than possession. That's not true for books. If you've ever felt that warmth in the stomach, that burst of excitement in the region of the heart, that movement of the face—a small tic of the mouth, perhaps, a new line on the forehead, the eyes that search, that devour—just as you are finally holding the longed-for book, when you open it, cracking it but just a little so you can *hear* it, anyone who has experienced that moment of incomparable happiness will understand what I mean. Opening a book is one of the most exhilarating, the most incomparable experiences that a person can have in his life.

For a long time now, I'd had my eye on the beautiful volumes in the bookstores on Mont-Royal or Sainte-Catherine Street, but this one was the first that was my very own. It was soft to the touch, it smelled good, the print wasn't crowded on the page, the paper, while it wasn't fine, was of decent quality and showed that Les Éditions Rencontres was a serious business, there was a little taffeta ribbon sewn into the binding to use as a bookmark ... I'd known I was going to kiss it the minute I saw the parcel on the dining room table, I often did that with the books that I loved passionately, but never had I imagined that one day I would want to *bite* a book.

The first of the three Greek plays was *Agamemnon*, by Aeschylus. Everything I knew about the Trojan war at that time I'd learned in *Helen of Troy*, a bad American movie by Robert Wise, shot in Italy and deadly dull, that I'd seen at the Palace a year before; it had starred Rosanna Podesta, Jacques Sernas and Brigitte Bardot in one of her first appearances on screen. So I knew about the abduction of Helen and its consequences on the lives of the Achaeans and the Trojans, because it had all been recounted in a hodgepodge of battle scenes and pages from history poorly strung together, but I knew practically nothing about what had come before the story of the Trojan horse or about the happy Atreus family: the true thirst for revenge of Menelaus and Agamemnon, Iphigenia's monstrous sacrifice, Clytemnestra's hysteria when one of her daughters was snatched away from her, the arrival of Aegisthus into the life of the queen, the disgrace of Electra and, most of all, the fate of the Trojan women after the victory of the Greeks. And so I began my reading totally ignorant not only of Greek history, but also of the fundamental rules of Greek theatre.

Already though I was madly in love with theatre. I gorged myself on all the TV dramas that Radio-Canada was producing at the time: sitting with my mother in front of the set, a glass of Nestlé's Quik in one hand and a Royal cake in the other. Every Thursday and Sunday evening I devoured Marcel Dubé and Molière, Chekhov and Françoise Loranger, Oscar Wilde and Félix Leclerc, Turgenev, Labiche, Hugo and Anne Hébert. Even Gabriel Arout and Jean-Robert Rémillard. I changed period, tone and style with wild abandon; I fretted about the heroine of *Lady Windermere's Fan*, who'd made the mistake of writing a message on her instrument, exploded with laughter at the garden scene in Georges Dandin, shed bitter tears over the misfortunes of Huguette Oligny in *A Month in the Country*, was spellbound by the language, so close to my own, of the characters in *Zone*, who could have been my neighbours, despite their names, amazing for Montrealers: Ciboulette (Green Onion), Tarzan, Moineau (Sparrow). But was I ready for Aeschylus?

I read three or four times the first monologue by the watchman posted on the ramparts of Argos before I could really grasp all of it: I looked up in my Larousse the names *Atreides, Argos, Ilion, Agamemnon,* I analyzed the text the way I'd been taught to do in school, parsing the complicated sentences, I reflected on the metaphors, on certain phrasing, certain images. And when I was convinced that I really did understand it all, I re-read the monologue aloud, and tears came to my eyes. So much was expressed in so few words, barely one printed page! The watchman who explained to us with magnificent images that for years he had been posted on the ramparts of Argos, waiting for news about the fall of Troy: I could see him and hear him. He spoke about the ineluctably changing seasons, about how badly Argos had been governed since the departure of the king, about Agamemnon's wife, the terrible Clytemnestra, who had dared to take a lover, who would rise to announce the fall of Troy to the inhabitants of the city, about how he, a simple watchman, wanted to leave the ramparts, to sing and dance to celebrate the victory of his people in a foreign land, all expressed so poetically that I spent a good hour re-reading the monologue, memorizing it:

> I ask the gods some respite from the weariness
> of this watchtime measured by years I lie awake
> elbowed upon the Atreidae's roof dogwise to mark
> the grand processionals of all the stars of night
> burdened with winter and again with heat for men,
> dynasties in their shining blazoned on the air,
> these stars, upon their wane and when the rest arise.

The beauty of those words! It was like nothing I knew, nothing I could recognize or comprehend, but once I'd finished analyzing it, once I had grasped the sense of the words, what joy overflowed from my heart! A breath of grandeur passed through my soul, once again I was travelling from Cartier Street in Montreal, but that day it was on the wings of a genius from over two thousand years ago, whose existence, whose stunning power I'd never have imagined if my brother Jacques hadn't signed up with Les Éditions Rencontres!

Why had no one ever talked about Aeschylus in school? Was he reserved for the privileged few who attended the classical colleges? Were we working-class children unworthy of him? Did we deserve nothing better than *La Perle au fond du gouffre* or *Les Anciens Canadiens*?

I moved on to the first chorus. The monologue was tricky but I eventually understood it as well as I did the watchman's. The entrance of the chorus though amazed me—I was used to opera choruses that I howled along with, driving my mother crazy when I listened to my records: "Gloire immortelle de nos aïeuuuuux!" or "Va pensieeeero, sull'alli della libertàààààà!" but what was the meaning of this chorus that was spoken?—and it took me a lot longer to understand the role played by these inhabitants of Argos who were leaving the city to come and talk to us. But when I began to guess at their utility, their function in the play, I was mesmerized, frozen there, struck down by a revelation that would change my life.

Instead of having a single narrator, as in a novel or in certain plays, Tennessee Williams's *The Glass Menagerie*, for instance, a group of citizens of Argos came out of the city to tell us what had happened before the play began, what we needed to know about the action, the places, the characters. That group was also the confidant of the characters and was itself a protagonist integrated into the action of the play. At school we'd been vaguely told about the three rules of the-atre: the unity of place, time, and action, with Corneille's *Polyeucte* as an example, probably because it was a Christian play, but we'd never been told how the ancient Greeks had invented and perfected those three rules by using as a binding, as a kind of cement, those many characters who formed a single one.

As I read the two other plays in the volume, which were not the last two sections of the *Oresteia*, I realized on my own—and this would be one of the great discoveries of my life—that in the theatre, when a character speaks about his woes in a monologue, only he is involved and the audience becomes his confidant, but that when several characters say the same thing at the same time as a chorus, they aren't added up, they are multiplied; they are no longer five or thirteen or twenty, they become a single character who represents and speaks for everyone. I had just discovered that it was possible to make an entire community speak in a single, multiple voice, in the same way that they're made to sing in an opera! And that operas, when all's said and done, are Greek tragedies that are sung.

I would see my first Greek tragedy a few years later, at the Théâtre du Nouveau Monde: *The Libation Bearers*, by Aeschylus, which is the continuation of the *Agamemnon* that I'd just read, a magnificent production directed by Jean-Pierre Ronfard, with Dyne Mousso, Albert Millaire, Charlotte Boisjoli and Nicole Fillion, a performance that unfortunately was misunderstood and went nearly unnoticed. But at the final performance—before an audi-ence of eleven in a house that seated a thousand—I would think: "That's it, theatre is what I want to do!" and I would remember reading *Agamemnon* and that production of *The Libation Bearers*, in 1965, when I wrote my first play in *joual*.

After I'd finished *Agamemnon*—I'd spent the whole after-noon reading it because there were many things I hadn't grasped on first reading—I had the impression that in a few hours I had grown, developed, become someone else, that I'd caught a glimpse of possibilities that would affect me personally and transform my life definitively; I didn't know yet what it would be, but I knew that it had entered my body, my heart, and would be there for the rest of my life.

I'd just been bitten by Greek literature and the next year, I would spend all summer delving into my brother's books— I didn't yet have access to the adults' room in the Municipal Library—searching for the stories of the Atreidae and of the Trojans. So there was something grand then, something significant behind the story of the Trojan horse? Who was the real Cassandra, the slave and mistress Agamemnon had brought home from Troy? What was Aegisthus doing in the queen's bed? And what about the massacre at the end, that unimaginable violence by two lovers who murdered the husband and his mistress? Would they be punished? Would the chorus who saw everything denounce them? I would learn everything about that family of psychopaths—Electra, Orestes, Chrysotemis—but this time thanks to the opera, when I acquired my first work by Richard Strauss: *Elektra*, the famous recording by Karl Böhm, with Inge Borkh.

I closed the book very gently, stroked it with the palm of my right hand as if to leave my warmth there—and I bit it with a sensual pleasure I've rarely experienced since.

My mother yelled; Jacques would be furious; a new book! with teeth marks!—but too bad, Greek tragedy already bore my mark!

BUG-JARGAL

Victor Hugo

Let's call him Brother Léon, because I've forgotten his name—or chosen to forget it. Brother Léon was my Grade Ten French teacher at the École secondaire Saint-Stanislas, the famous E.S.S.S., renowned throughout Quebec for its corps of cadets and buglers (oh yes, for three years I was in the E.S.S.S. cadet corps and every minute of it was a nightmare!). Brother Léon liked me because he thought I had talent, and he was strict with me for the same reason. He didn't let me get away with anything and the smallest mistake in composition or dictation cost me more than it would anyone else in the three Grade Ten classes. When I complained about his severity—as I sometimes did in the face of certain flagrant acts of injustice—he would reply: "With your talent, Tremblay, I ought to give you zero automatically when you make a grammatical error or don't pay attention!"

He encouraged me to write, suspected that I already did, and complained that I never showed him anything.

"Your compositions are very good but I'd give anything to know what else you're up to! Are you ashamed of what you write when you're alone at home? Because I'm convinced, Tremblay, that you write in secret!"

I went red, but admitted nothing because I intended to keep quiet about the subjects I dealt with: after all, I wasn't going to tell him that I'd just finished a homosexual novel, or a fantastic tale inspired by the Virgin of Nuremberg, in which a medieval baron imprisoned women in iron robes, then roasted and ate them! But he must have suspected something, because he saw me blush, with obvious satisfaction.

At home, I'd run out of hiding places for my writing, which was growing at lightning speed. My brother's red Atlas, where for a long time I'd concealed my first poems, wasn't safe any more: it was the only book in the house whose spine was never covered with dust, which meant that my mother "visited" it regularly. Needless to say there was no question of using one of the drawers in Jacques's desk or my bedside table—I'd inherited Bernard's bedroom furniture when he married the wonderful Monique, of whom my mother always said, with a little smile, "He's a lucky boy, he doesn't deserve her!"—too easy a target for, let's say, someone who walked around the house regularly with a can of Pledge and a damp cloth.

But at the time when these events were taking place, I'd just invented a subterfuge I thought was as ingenious as the one in Edgar Allan Poe's "Purloined Letter," no less.

I'd quickly realized that Jacques didn't really read the books he bought from Les Éditions Rencontres. He leafed through them when they arrived, read a few passages, then put them in the bookcase where they'd have gone yellow and never been opened again had I not devoured them.

Some months earlier, I had started writing a series of fantastic tales inspired by Poe, as it happens, and by Jean Ray, Nerval and H.P. Lovecraft, a turn-of-the-century American writer that I dreamed secretly was my grand-father, because I'd read somewhere that he had visited the brothels of Providence around the beginning of the twentieth century, at the time when some malicious gossips claimed that my maternal grandmother had "lived the life."

In my dream, Lovecraft met Maria Desrosiers in the brothel, fell madly in love with her, asked her not to take precautions when they made love, and had a child with her: *my mother!* That made me Lovecraft's grandson and I would carry the torch of the fantastic tale that he'd held so high! I hid my own stories in one of the Éditions Rencontres books. And so the four volumes of *The Brothers Karamazov*, the two volumes of *The Idiot*, the beautiful padded editions of *Tess of the Durbervilles* and *L'Assommoir* each contained one of my tales, folded in four, and I was positive no one would go looking for them because they were too easy to find.

The fact remains that one fine day, Brother Léon decided to deliver a lengthy diatribe about the books on the Index. It was rather surprising, because aside from me almost no one in the class was a serious reader. We were in the science class, and the arts in general and literature in particular weren't held in very high esteem.

I thought his speech was funny because it was more like a list of recommended reading than an irrevocable condemnation of writers who had dared to create reprehensible works. For instance, he said: "Now listen to me, I want you to understand that all of Victor Hugo is on the Index! He was a writer with dissolute ways who claimed to be close to God but who practised revolution more than religion! Don't even go near his books, all you need to read is a brief excerpt from *Les Travailleurs de la mer*, which you'll be asked to analyze in your French classes. Do not read his poetry! Do not read his novels! They are all pernicious works!"

He certainly made us want to read Hugo, even the biggest dunces who'd never opened a book in their lives. Maybe that was what he'd intended.

I had just finished *Notre-Dame de Paris*, in the small Nelson collection, and I couldn't understand what was so reprehensible about it. I'd been thrilled by the long passages about the print shop, which was, Hugo said, the greatest human invention since the wheel. When I gave them to my father to read, they'd brought tears to his eyes, I had wanted to mother Quasimodo, whose plight moved me, and I'd thought Esméralda was ridiculous with her goat and her too-handsome boyfriend ... It was a book that made me want to leave Montreal and go to read the façade of Notre Dame cathedral in Paris as if it were an open book, an endless volume that would reveal to me all the mysteries of the Middle Ages. How could a Catholic teaching brother condemn such a book?

Because of the dissolute ways Brother Léon had mentioned, I suppose. After all, wasn't Esméralda a *bohemian* who, we could assume, had lost her virginity long ago and slept around? I watched my classmates, who drank in the teacher's words while they took notes ... All of it, the reeking hypocrisy, the devious way of giving us the urge to read, if that was Brother's intention, which was far from certain, was so ridiculous! Why not simply say that *Notre-Dame de Paris* was a novel that was easy to read, more fascinating than a western, and infinitely gratifying to the soul? Why not try to encourage reading for positive reasons, rather than through the lure of a possible sin?

In the middle of Brother Léon's diatribe against the books on the Index, I realized for the first time that what I was writing was probably "reprehensible." Dostoevsky and Tolstoy and Zola, who were certainly on the Index too, were serving as hiding places for other writing that was just as deserving of blame! I couldn't help laughing, which brought down the teacher's wrath.

"Stand up, Tremblay, and tell us what's so funny! Come on! Stand up and let us see how nice and red your face is! So the Index makes you laugh, does it? I suppose you don't think it concerns you. Maybe you even read those books! Do you? Do you read them? Do you read books on the Index, yes or no?"

I replied without thinking: "I read *Notre-Dame de Paris* but I didn't know it was on the Index ... "

Shocked murmurs, the teacher bracing himself. I think, Oh boy, I've just signed my own death warrant, what an idiot! He comes up to me, redder than I was a minute before, with a stick in hand, ready to strike.

"You read *Notre-Dame de Paris!*"

"That's right."

"The whole thing?"

"That's right."

"Did you confess?"

"I just told you, I didn't know it was on the Index ... "

"Keep quiet! Lower your eyes! Do an act of contrition!"

"I can't do an act of contrition *after* I found out the book was on the Index, Brother, I didn't commit a sin!"

"Don't be a smart aleck! You're going to the principal's office right now, and you're going to ask for special permission to confess *immediately!* Tell him it's extremely important!"

"He's going to think I've killed somebody!"

"I told you to keep quiet!"

He turned towards the others.

"See what happens when you read Victor Hugo? It makes you arrogant! You're really letting me down, Tremblay! I thought that you had some common sense, that you were a good Catholic. I'm beginning to seriously wonder if I even feel like reading what you write on the sly. I don't imagine it's very nice!"

In a few minutes the incident had made the rounds of the school. Tremblay in Grade Ten C had read Victor Hugo and he'd had to go and confess right away. I was so humiliated as I went to the church—as soon as I'd confessed my offence, the principal had phoned the presbytery to ask that my confession be heard at once—that I wished I could die then and there, disappear between the cracks in the sidewalk, risking Hell if I really was in a state of mortal sin. Then the childishness of the whole episode made me smile. And I swore that I'd try to get my revenge.

***

It was the most hilarious confession of my brief career as a practising Catholic. A priest was waiting for me at the door of Saint-Stanislas Church, thinking I'd committed some ignominious sin, probably licking his lips before he even heard what I had to say.

He led the way, rustling down the lateral aisle that led to the confessionals. I thought he looked quite handsome in his soutane—he'd pulled it up with a belt to go skating and I could see the bottom of his pants—and I tried to look elsewhere. After all, I didn't want to have a real sin to confess! Especially not one involving him!

"For the love of God, what did you do to interrupt our Wednesday afternoon hockey game?"

"I read Victor Hugo."

He stopped short, turned towards me.

"I read *Notre-Dame de Paris*, by Victor Hugo."

"Is that all?"

"That's right. Apparently it's enough."

"The principal of the E.S.S.S. interrupts me so I can hear your confession because you've read *Notre-Dame de Paris*, by Victor Hugo?"

"That's right."

"He's an imbecile!"

"It's on the Index ... "

He brought his hand to his hair and fiddled with it nervously. His hair was gorgeous ...

"It is? *Notre-Dame de Paris* is on the Index? I didn't know that."

148

"But it is."

"Did *you* know?"

"Uh uh ... If *you* didn't know ... "

"You didn't commit a sin if you didn't know! But ... did you commit any sins when you were reading it?"

"Umm ... I don't know ... no, I don't think so."

"What an idiot! Go back to school at once, I'll deal with your principal ... But say a few Hail Mary's just in case ... "

We hadn't even got to the confessional.

Brother Léon watched me come into the classroom and in place of his eyes there were two loaded rifles, ready to fire. He and the principal must have heard from the hockey-playing priest while I was on my way back to school. He had wanted to teach me a lesson but he'd only managed to make himself look ridiculous and drag his principal to the abyss along with him.

But he didn't know yet what was waiting for him. Neither did I, for that matter, because I was going to pay dearly for one of the most courageous acts of my teenage years.

***

My brother had been teaching French for years so he possessed the valuable and mystical "teachers' book," the famous publication of the Department of Public Education that contained all the answers to all the French exercises from Grade One to Grade Twelve, and which I boasted I'd never consulted. I often saw it lying on Jacques's desk, hundreds of times I could have looked up the answers to the hardest assignments, but as I wasn't a cheat by nature and, as all my friends and family knew, I was extremely pig-headed, I preferred to look for them on my own, cursing, and find them, exultant. Or let myself sink into despair if I couldn't.

That day though I had a reason to consult it and I talked to my brother as soon as he got home from school.

"Since when have you been snooping in my teachers' book?"

"Never, I swear, but now I want to look up something and I'd rather ask your permission ... "

"What is it you're looking for? Maybe I can help you."

"I'm looking for the writers on the Index."

Jacques threw back his head and laughed.

"That's easy: probably anything you want to read is on it!"

"I'm serious! I want to look at the list of novels by Victor Hugo."

"I let you read *Notre-Dame de Paris* and didn't say anything, but don't go overboard."

"I just want to read the list to see if they're all on the Index."

"I'm sure they are but you won't find it in the teachers' book."

I'd stirred his curiosity; I was saved. He took out a big book that I hadn't seen before, the *Book of the Index* by a man called Sagehomme, but whether he was wise enough to live up to his name was another matter ... Jacques leafed quickly through the book, like someone used to consulting this kind of publication, then came out with a victorious cry.

"Here it is! See, what did I tell you?"

Victor Hugo took up an entire page. I was deeply disappointed: *Notre-Dame de Paris*, *Les Misérables*, *Quatre-vingt-treize*, all condemned, forbidden ... Furious, I was about to close the book when I noticed a short paragraph at the bottom of the page. It said that Hugo's first novel, *Bug-Jargal*, which he'd written at sixteen and which we happened to have a copy of, again in the small and attractive Nelson collection, *was not on the Index!* I had my revenge!

My brother took back the book.

"You're too happy, I'm sure you're up to something!"

***

With a boldness I don't think I have today, I showed up in class the next day with my copy of *Bug-Jargal*, which I hadn't even started to read.

In high school the last period of the day, from three twenty-five until four fifteen, if I remember correctly, was free: we could read or do homework or prepare for the next day's classes. I liked that period but nobody else did, because in general the other pupils hated to read, do homework or prepare for the next day's classes. I suppose that without knowing it, for the others I was the worst kind of brown-noser.

That day—it had been a fairly good one for me: despite my unpopularity, because I was good in French and was considered, rightly or wrongly, to be Brother Léon's pet, my classmates had asked what it was that had made the teacher act so mean the day before, and several times I'd treated myself to a detailed account of my visit to the church—that day, then, at three twenty-five, I brazenly took *Bug-Jargal* out of my desk, held it up so the teacher could see it clearly— Brother Léon was our home-room teacher and supervised our free period—and with my head down and brow furrowed I pretended to be reading.

Before long Brother Léon took the bait and less than five minutes later he came up to my desk and casually looked over my shoulder so he could read the title of my book.

"VICTOR HUGO!"

My twenty-nine classmates were startled, some even gave little cries of surprise because it was the first time we'd heard Brother Léon raise his voice so much. All heads turned in our direction.

Brother Léon was livid. He had cried out the name of the author of *Bug-Jargal* the way you expel air from your lungs after a punch in the belly, but he couldn't speak and I thought he was going to collapse beside my desk, dead of apoplexy.

He grabbed me by the scruff of the neck, lifted me, and dragged me to the door. We covered the distance between the classroom and the principal's office in record time. I was still holding the book when we entered the office.

The explanation was long, gruelling, and uncontrolled and, in the end, humiliating. Systematic humiliation of the pupils was the main specialty, the tremendous power of the Brothers of Christian Education; that day, I had proof of it once again. I won because I could prove that *Bug-Jargal* wasn't on the Index, but they represented authority and exploited it liberally: they accused me of being pretentious, of having a swelled head, of being as stubborn as a mule; they threatened to kick me out of school as an undesirable—I could already see my mother, who was always boasting about my classroom success, mortified to death—they claimed I was a bad influence on the other pupils because I only talked to Réal Bastien whom I'd known for six years, and Jean-Claude Hamel, who was one of the only nice guys in the class; they made me get down on my knees with my gaze lowered all the time they were showering me with insults.

I had dared to stand up to them; worse, I had dared to be right when they were wrong, and they intended to make me pay. I left the office feeling groggy, depressed, and furious despite my victory, and a little worried about my future at Saint-Stanislas Secondary School.

They could go on humiliating me, but they couldn't stop me from reading *Bug-Jargal* and I read it in class, a few chapters every day, all the way to the end, under the hate-filled eyes of Brother Léon, who claimed that he couldn't get over my ingratitude towards him who had until then considered me to be a model student.

Need I add that my marks in French felt the effects in spite of my efforts to improve my compositions and my obsessive attention to making as few mistakes as possible in dictation?

One more injustice meant nothing to them and they made the most of it. For the first time in years and for a period of months, I didn't lead the class in French. My mother frowned when she got my report card, and she signed it without asking any questions, but I could tell that I was letting her down and, gnawed by guilt, I consigned my disgrace deep down in my heart. I wasn't going to be a tattletale too!

But I consoled myself very quickly by reading the complete novels of Victor Hugo.

ORAGE SUR MON CORPS (A Storm Over My Body)

André Béland

It was one of those real March snowstorms, nasty and violent and wet, and it left on the ground the depressing brown slush made up of snow, sand and salt, half-ice and half-mud, that's the despair of Montrealers every spring. Even children, who can't do a thing with this mess, who are soaked to the bones after just a few minutes, hate this kind of snow and stay inside.

As usual at that time of year, the forecast had called it the storm of the century, but what fell on us was actually just the nightmare of the month. We'd seen worse in February but minus the slush, because it had been cold.

Every Friday afternoon when school got out, I would board the de la Roche trolley just across the street and go to the Municipal Library. It drove along Parc Lafontaine, then went south along Amherst Street to what we called "the bottom of town." On the day in question—it was Thursday and I'll explain why later on—because of the snow that was falling and the brown, frozen mud that hadn't started to melt yet, the huge vehicle was struggling, skidding, sliding, generously spraying passers-by already soaked to the underwear, who shook their fists at it.

The trolley bus was a strange compromise between street-car and bus, a bus that was electrified like a streetcar, actually, and I'd never understood why it had been invented:

it shook up its passengers like an ordinary bus and like the streetcar was at the mercy of power failures; it was noisy; it gave off showers of sparks at intersections; you felt as if it was charging at you when it drew up to the sidewalk to take on passengers, then drove off again too quickly, stopping too abruptly; it had all the drawbacks of the other two means of transportation and no advantages of its own. As for me, it made me carsick and I would have avoided it if I could. But my Friday afternoons were devoted to the library and the trolley bus was the only way to get there unless I wanted to walk.

That day, it was unbearably hot inside so the windows were foggy, the passengers grumpy, and I was furious at having decided to go to the library on Thursday instead of Friday. But I had a good reason.

***

During the last two years that I was restricted to the children's room, I'd pleaded with the librarians to make an exception, to let me go to the adults' room one floor up. Because after six years of tireless attendance I'd read everything that interested me and I was fed up with taking out the same old books week after week. True, I devoured the ones that Jacques received from Les Éditions Rencontres, but the adult room in the Municipal Library signified so much more: it meant total freedom of choice. I could read all of Zola's *Rougon-Macquart*, not just *L'Assommoir*, all of Balzac's *La Comédie humaine*, not just *Le Père Goriot*, and most of all, Proust's *À la recherche du temps perdu*, which I was dying to read.

But they categorically refused to grant my wish: no *child* had ever been allowed to go up to the adults' room, the rules weren't about to be changed overnight, and that was that.

I'd been very excited then at the approach of my sixteenth birthday. I counted the weeks, the days, I hardly slept the night before, and when June 25, 1958 finally arrived I'd gone to the adults' room that very morning to fill out my first forms.

What a feast!

Following the example of my Grandmother Tremblay, in my hunger for reading I devoured both Bazin and Balzac, Robert Choquette and Musset, Anouilh and Shakespeare, Pierre Benoit and Camus, Christie and Sand—without discrimination, making choices that weren't always the right ones, I suppose, but it didn't matter, I had inexplicable attractions and a passion for reading that my mother claimed was close to mental illness.

"Reading's all well and good, I've always encouraged you, but your skull's going to explode! You'll go blind! You'll be the size of an elephant, you don't move for days at a time! It's a beautiful day, go outside for a while!"

"Mama, the things they make us read in school put me to sleep. I want to get a proper education. When I go back in September, I want to be a person who knows something besides the scene with Trissotin in *Les Femmes savantes* and that stupid speech about the nose!"

"You already know something else ... "

"But not enough!"

"You aren't reading too many things that are forbidden, are you?"

"No, not too many ... "

Yes, too many. But they were so wonderful! To discover Camus by yourself, suspect there's a hidden meaning behind the story in *The Plague*, leaf through the papers, read the book reviews, jump for joy when you find out that you were right, that the rats were more than rats ...

The summer passed in a constantly renewed euphoria: six books every two weeks and not easy ones; endless discussions with Ginette Rouleau, Claude Sauvé, Richard Desrosiers, Gérard Sanchis; unexpected discoveries that knocked me out; aversions that surprised me, that I couldn't explain to myself: why was I allergic to the dry but beautiful prose of André Gide while Proust's tangled sentences thrilled me so, even if they were so complicated that I couldn't always find my way in them?

A guy I'd met in Parc Lafontaine one night—that summer, my sex life was nearly as active as my reading, Mama was wrong to think I wasn't getting any exercise—had told me about a "homosexual" Quebec novel that had come out during the war with the quite simple title *Orage sur mon corps*. Curious to see what it was all about, I decided to borrow it from the library, if they had a copy. I thought the title was rather pompous and ridiculous, but a homosexual Quebec novel—that was something I had to read!

I had a surprise in store.

I remember very clearly that the first time I filled out the slip for *Orage sur mon corps*, I was with Ginette Rouleau. We were the same age, we'd been "promoted" to the adults' room at nearly the same time, and we were spending the summer when we'd turned sixteen in either Parc Lafontaine or on the Rouleaus' balcony on Fabre Street, reading forbidden books that we loved. Suspecting that homosexual novels weren't looked on kindly, I hid my slip among other, less compromising ones: some Agatha Christies, a Pierre Benoit, a Mauriac—though Mauriac ...

The librarians always went through our slips before they left the room, probably to make sure they were in order so as not to waste time or take too many needless steps.

Needless to say I landed on the strictest one, who happened to be the oldest and was probably a fine person but whose face tended to express what she thought of our reading choices as she was going through our slips. My heart was thumping when I gave her mine, which she began to fiddle with, shuffling them as if they were playing cards. When she got to *Orage sur mon corps*, she stopped dead, put the slip aside on the counter and stared at me for some very long seconds, then snapped: "That one's out!"

She didn't even bother pretending to look for the book, she had *decided*, by herself, that it was out! She was refusing to give it to me!

I blushed to my toenails.

She stared at me for quite a while before she went back to my other slips, and I thought I was going to faint from shame.

At the time, I didn't talk about my homosexuality, I didn't want to hurt my parents or my friends, who might not have understood, so this was the first time I'd felt myself being judged on the matter. What I read in the librarian's expression truly horrified me: disgust, contempt and even, yes, even hatred.

I couldn't confide in Ginette, who had no idea what was going on, and I leaned against the counter to keep from falling.

"What's wrong? You look as if you're about to explode!"

"I don't know—I guess it's the heat."

This was the beginning of a kind of silent struggle between the old librarian and me. So she wanted to judge me, did she? Very well, she was going to get a chance to do just that!

Every time I went to the library that summer, that fall and over a good part of the winter, I filled out a slip for *Orage sur mon corps*. I waited for my librarian to be free, I went up to her and handed her my pile of forms, looking her squarely in the eye. And every time, she met my gaze, put the slip aside without looking at it, and told me: "That one's out," then went away with the others. Whether I read the book or not no longer mattered, I wanted to vanquish this dragon of the Municipal Library and I'd take as long as I needed to do it!

My doggedness turned against me, of course. One Friday after school that winter, she told me, carefully articulating each syllable: "That book's out and for you, it always will be! So you can quit being so stubborn!"

It was censorship and I knew it. I was sixteen years old and I believed that I had the right to read whatever I wanted, but I had absolutely no idea how to defend myself. Besides that, I'd trapped myself: we'd go on playing the little game as long as I persisted and I could sense that she wouldn't let me have the book till I was twenty-one, when she had no alternative. And even so! She could go on claiming that it was out just to piss me off! But I dug my heels in, determined that I wouldn't buy the book, that I'd get my hands on the library copy, and nothing would make me give up.

I finally learned, I don't remember how, that my favourite librarian didn't work on Thursday, and that was why I was on the La Roche trolley bus, in the middle of a snowstorm on a day other than Friday.

***

The library was deserted. I was the only person in Montreal crazy enough to travel through part of the city in a snowstorm, on a trolley bus besides, in search of André Béland's *Orage sur mon corps!*

The three young and pretty librarians were gossiping, leaning against the wooden tables that served as desks or sitting on those uncomfortable straight chairs whose purpose I was understanding for the first time, because usually the library employees were either looking at the slips filled out by subscribers or had gone to the upper floors of the building to look for the books requested.

All three watched me go to the little wooden drawers. I was aware that three pairs of young girl's eyes were scrutinizing me and I felt as if I were walking strangely. I hoped—and this was the first time in my life that it had happened and I felt deeply humiliated—I hoped I didn't look too effeminate. I headed straight for the letter B. I thought I could see them out of the corner of my eye, giggling, but I wasn't sure; I mustn't be paranoid, after all, the entire city of Montreal didn't know I'd been trying for months to get that book!

As usual, I concealed the slip for *Orage sur mon corps* among others I cared about less—I think I even descended so low as to ask for something by Berthe Bernage, whom I couldn't stand, just to soften up the girl in case she knew what was in Béland's book—and then, gathering my courage, I went up to the counter.

The youngest girl, who was closest to me, held out her hand, smiling—whew! I'd panicked over nothing—took the books that I was bringing back, stamped them, picked up the slips and studied them while her colleagues looked on, squirming on their chairs. Maybe they played the same little game whenever a young man turned up ... When she got to *Orage sur mon corps* though, she stiffened a little, turned red all at once, looked at the other two librarians as if to ask, What do I do? then said to me, more gently than the dragon but without looking at me: "I'm sorry, that book is out."

I swallowed, making a noise that must have been heard all the way to Sherbrooke Street. What to do? I couldn't run away. I had to say something. Absolutely. Cry censorship? Show them, at any rate, or pretend, rather, that I wasn't afraid.

"Tell me, is it only out when *I* want to borrow it? I've been asking for it for months!"

She was still looking down at the slip as if she didn't know what to do with it.

"It's always out, as you say, for men under twenty-one. On management orders."

All at once I was so furious that I could have jumped over the counter and strangled her. I wasn't afraid now, I wasn't ashamed, I was steaming! But it wasn't her fault, she was doing as she'd been told. The excuse was threadbare but effective, so I was helpless. I leaned across to her.

"You mean a woman could take it out?"

"Not very many ask for it ... "

"But if I was a girl of my age you'd let me have it?"

"I suppose so."

"So if I put '-lle' at the end of my name ... "

"Look, I know you're a guy ... "

"But you won't get caught, the slip will say I'm a girl!"

"Don't push it, I'm not allowed to do that!"

I grabbed the slips from her.

"Never mind, I'll do without it!"

And I left with all the dignity I could muster.

The only one who could have saved me then was Ginette Rouleau, but I wasn't ready to share my secret with her.

And that's why I've never read *Orage sur mon corps!*

VOL DE NUIT (Night Flight)

Antoine de Saint-Exupéry

Before I get into this story that had as great an influence on me as my discovery of Greek tragedy, I'd liked to tell you about something that drove me wild with jealousy around thirty years ago.

As we did every night after a show, some friends and I were eating at Giuseppe's, an excellent Italian restaurant on Notre-Dame Street that was popular with the Montreal theatre community from the late sixties till the mid-seventies.

That evening, we'd been joined—"we" being the noisy, not always discerning but always laughing nucleus of our merry band of young revellers: André Brassard, who was reluctantly learning to eat something besides hamburgers; Claude Gai, who joined me every evening in savouring a dish of pasta carbonara; the wonderful Denyse Filiatraut, as usual hurrying to eat so she could go and keep an eye on her own restaurant; Christine Olivier; Robert L., my boyfriend at the time; John Goodwin, who was already watching over us like a mother; and Camille who told me now and then: "Don't eat too much Michel, or you'll be chewing Diovol all night!"—we'd been joined, then, by the poet and playwright Michel Garneau and the actress Michelle Rossignol, who'd just taken up again, brilliantly, the role of Pierrette Guérin in *Les Belles-Soeurs* (this was 1971).

We were telling stories about our childhood, Brassard's on Des Érables Street, Denyse's on Cartier, John's in Quebec City, Camille's in Chicoutimi, mine on Fabre Street, which I was already plundering shamelessly, when Michel Garneau started telling us that once, when he was very young, a French gentleman had come to visit his parents in Quebec City. One day the French gentleman sat the boy on his knees and began to describe a book he was writing, the story of a little prince who lived on a tiny planet along with a rose, a snake and a fox ... The rest of us were stunned. He'd been told the story of *Le Petit Prince* by Saint-Exupéry himself! Michel had sat on the lap of Antoine de Saint-Exupéry! What was he like? Kind? Mean? Pretentious? Modest? Did he think he was a great writer, or was he unaffected like a real one? Did he drink as much as people said? And when he'd been drinking, did he cut off people's neckties as legend claimed?

A silence followed his answers, which were abundant, apt and warm as always—Michel is a great raconteur—and then I'd declared that the only celebrity I had ever sighted as a child was Ginette Raynault (before she changed it to Reno), who was raising hell all over the parish and whom I ran into now and then, not daring to speak to her because she was already an imposing figure, at the Centre Immaculée-Conception.

As usual, I'd drowned my uneasiness—my jealousy, actually, a real attack of the kind that squeezes your heart, that stabs and numbs your solar plexus—in self-mockery.

***

I remember a horrible flu, complete with blocked sinuses, head full of cotton batting, nose raw from handkerchiefs even though they were soft from countless hand-washings, I remember it was a bright spring day but that I had trouble seeing because my eyes smarted so much, I remember my mother's inevitable chicken soup, and a paperback book that lay spine-up on my bed.

This was a few months after the incident with *Orage sur mon corps*. I hadn't really got over my humiliation and had started buying paperbacks so I wouldn't have to appear too often before those women I now called "my tormenters," and I was already proud of the fact that the third shelf from the bottom of the bookcase belonged to me: that was where I put everything I intended to read and suspected they wouldn't let me take out of the library: Wilde, Proust, Genêt, *The Satyricon*—all of them of course mixed in with other books so as not to attract my brother's or my mother's suspicion. My adventures with the dragon of the Municipal Library had proven to be a good thing in the end, because I was learning to treasure my own books. I looked at my shelf in the bookcase and thought: "Those books are all mine, I didn't borrow even one!"

Very few were new and none had a padded cover, but they were mine!

My own stories had moved and now I was folding the paper in eight before I buried them between the loving pages of *The Portrait of Dorian Gray*, the demonic dialogues in *Les Bonnes* or the famous orgy in *The Satyricon*.

I'd come across *Vol de nuit* in a pile of old cut-price paperbacks on the mezzanine at Dupuis Frères. Ten cents a book, three for a quarter. I had liked *Le Petit Prince* when I was a child, but I'd read nothing else by Saint-Exupéry, maybe because he was held in such high esteem by the Brothers of Christian Education ...

And that morning, laid low by the flu, I chose *Vol de nuit* because of its big type and few pages. A quick and easy read, perfect for a day with the flu. I didn't have an inkling about the surprise that was waiting for me, or that I would be a different person before the day was over.

I read *Vol de nuit* three times that day. Actually, I read the whole book twice and the third time I went back to the passages that had impressed me most, underlining whole pages, jotting comments in the margins, turning down corners to find them more easily.

I'd never before read a novel that didn't really tell a story and at first I wasn't sure what to think of it. Three planes leave from three godforsaken places in South America to bring mail from Europe to Buenos Aires, a smug boss, a spineless and toadying inspector, a storm: okay, fine, but what's the story? And then the beauty of the landscapes described—in the first chapter they're flying over Patagonia instead of crossing it like the characters in *Les Enfants du capitaine Grant* and I felt as if I were soaring above the Cordillera of the Andes, the sun setting behind me as the menacing, mysterious night approaches; the palpable, sensual atmosphere of this account that instead of telling an ordinary story, was making us experience what the characters were feeling—the perfectly controlled resignation of Fabien, whose plane plunges into the sea; the love of the two women, combined with the fear of losing them, for their husbands, who are in constant danger because they're pioneers in commercial aviation at night; the exceptional way in which the author probed the soul of his protagonists, as if his pen were a scalpel; and the splendour of his style, above all his style, his very personal way of playing with the words, the sentences, soon had me pinned to my bed, forgetting about my flu and holding onto my book as if it were a kite that would let me soar to previously unknown heights.

For a long time I'd been rebelling during French class against the simplistic style we had to use in our compositions: subject, verb, object—in that order, if you please. As few inversions as possible, they muddle the meaning of the sentence, and no interpolated clauses: if we felt the need to put a few words between commas, it was probably because they belonged somewhere else, *in their proper place!*

I suppose it was good for the students—and they were the majority—who were bored senseless by writing compositions. But to me who loved to write, who already, alone in my corner, was writing fantastic tales in which I was trying to hide my doubts and misgivings, to me who had secret dreams of one day being published, these restrictions were deeply shocking, and even when I was hidden away in my corner, they kept me from functioning, from writing the way I wanted.

My teachers—even the dread Brother Léon—did let me stray now and then because they thought I had some talent for what they called "the proper use of the French language," but when I'd gone too far in their opinion, they would return my essays covered with red and with comments in the margins. "Do this again, it's not worthy of you." "Did you have a fever when you wrote this mess?" "Instead of wasting your time on *Notre-Dame de Paris* or *Bug-Jargal*, read Félix Leclerc!" " A *clear* soul expresses itself in *clear* language!" Yet they must have suspected, ever since the *Bug-Jargal* incident, that my soul was not clear and that I'd never want it to be!

Saint-Exupéry was not the first writer whose style I was aware of, of course, but his sentences—short and at the same time often boldly structured—were opening doors to me that the Brothers of Christian Education had kept carefully shut. For example, he wrote: "Robineau, standing beside him, with his eyes fixed on the map, was gradually pulling himself together," or this sentence, which I found particularly interesting: "In the quiet bed, as in a harbour, he was sleeping and, lest anything should spoil his rest, she smoothed out a little fold of sheet with her hand, bringing calm upon the bed, as a divine hand calms the sea." All the hesitation of the night pilot's wife who doesn't dare to waken her husband yet because she is afraid of losing him every time he leaves to deliver the mail from Europe, was in the very structure of the sentence as much as in the words chosen to express it. The parts of the sentence clashed, the series of commas interrupted the reader's thught, you could sense the anxiety, the nervousness of the woman who thought it was abnormal to waken her husband at such an hour—in the middle of the night—so he could fly across the Atlantic Ocean in the dark.

If I'd ever dared to construct a sentence like that, Brother Léon would probably have written in the margin: "Was that necessary? Straighten out that sentence! It's not a sentence, it's a puzzle!" Why did Saint-Exupéry have the right to circumvent the rules, so strict, of the French language and not me? I also wanted to turn it all upside down, to rattle the bars of the cage, to find a way that would become my own to turn around, while I used them, the laws that had been inculcated in me for ten years now. Whose usefulness I respected, though I didn't want to apply them to the letter in an endless drone of sentences that were well constructed but as dull as a rainy Sunday afternoon.

Vol de nuit was also the first book I read in which the central character is ultimately unsympathetic because of his uprightness, his refusal to make any concession, to admit any weakness: rarely have I loathed a character as much as I did Rivière, even though I understood his reasons for being what he was. Rivière's awareness that he was unfair and his self-justifications were like two waves of equal power that I was caught between, and even after three readings I couldn't find a way to reconcile them, to make them merge into each other. Intellectually, I understood why Rivière refused any feelings that were too human— sympathy, pity—that could get in the way of his men's productivity, but I refused to accept that a leader dismissed the admiration and even more, the friendship of the men he was guiding, only so that he could push them towards a perfection that was unattainable.

I was beginning vaguely to understand why the Brothers of Christian Education admired Saint-Exupéry so much—his humanitarian message was very close to certain Christian doctrines—but a marked difference irrevocably separated the great writer from my pathetic teachers: Saint-Exupéry's character was merciless towards his men out of love for humankind, out of his desire to see the human being surpass himself by crossing the ocean at *night* by plane, at a time when that wasn't done yet, whereas the Brothers of Christian Education were strict with us purely out of a need to humiliate us, to "teach us a lesson," to "make examples" of us, to transform us—despite ourselves if need be—into good Catholics, to make us experience the loathsome feeling that has always corrupted Catholicism: guilt. Always. Over everything. Everywhere.

I took out all the stories I'd written and hidden in my paperbacks and re-read them feverishly. I wasn't comparing them with Saint-Exupéry, needless to say, I wasn't that pretentious, I only wanted to see if I'd followed my teachers' directives too closely, if my style was too "ordinary," respectful of the rules, dull, and boring simply because I'd been told so often to watch out for boldness that I was afraid of it.

And as soon as I was over the flu, despite the relief that I'd felt on re-reading them—I thought they weren't all that bad—I began to rewrite my fantastic tales completely, this time letting myself give free rein to my imagination and trying not to think too much about my Grevisse grammar book while I wrote.

And when I felt an urge to write a new tale, I would put *Vol de nuit* on my desk. Without looking at it, of course, I wasn't trying to copy Saint-Exupéry, but just to back up my conviction that my teachers were wrong and that a brave friend was watching over me.

And so I developed two completely different styles: one for school, because I wanted my marks to remain high—and even more, because ever since the *Bug-Jargal* incident, it had been in my interest to keep quiet—the other, more baroque and infinitely more personal, just for myself, like a gift.

It gave what it gave, but at least it reflected me.

CONTES POUR BUVEURS ATTARDÉS
(Tales for Late Night Drinkers)

Michel Tremblay

Between the ages of sixteen and nineteen, I'd penned around forty fantastic tales brought together under the rather pompous and not very seductive title *Contes gothiques.*

This was obviously a nod to the Anglo-Saxon school of fiction called "Gothic novels," which was still very popular in the United States, particularly, it seemed, among women trying to escape from their humdrum lives by taking refuge in bewildering stories at the limit of the fantastic: love potions, family curses, violent or moaning ghosts, fabulous treasures, secrets jealously guarded and dramatically revealed, intermarriages that had stunning consequences, beautiful heroines, heroes even more gorgeous and, of course, happy endings. My own tales were definitely closer to Poe, Jean Ray, Lovecraft, Hoffmann, Stocker—authors who weren't "Gothic" at all and who lapsed into bloody horror, but I liked the title and tried to impress my gang with it. They resisted.

It was 1965, I'd just turned twenty-three and I had a manuscript that had been mouldering in my desk for three years now. But I hesitated to show it to a publisher, and my new friends André Brassard, Louise Jobin, François Laplante, and Ginette Lefebvre were starting to chide me, kindly but firmly, for not moving my ass to get them published. They were right of course, but the same sense of unworthiness that for years had kept me from submitting my play *Le Train* to the Radio-Canada Young Writers' Competition because I hadn't attended a classical college—a competition I'd finally won, in 1964, with that same play—still ate away at me and I simply couldn't take my stories, stuff them in an envelope, and address it to a publisher. Who did I think I was—me, a humble linotypist—wanting to impose my hesitant and ridiculous prose on the rest of the world? There were already enough writers starving to death! Besides, who would be interested in fantastic literature by a Québécois? Anyway, no one would be crazy enough to publish it and I wasn't strong enough yet to swallow a refusal, so why even try? Or dream? My dreams took me nowhere, I already had proof of that ...

There was no follow-up to Young Writers' Competition. I'd just finished a play, *Les Belles-Soeurs*, which Brassard was trying vainly to force on the few individuals he knew in Montreal theatre circles. Actually, the Dominion Drama Festival had just turned it down—two of the three judges had thought it was monstrous and vulgar—so I was beginning to think seriously about laying down my pen and devoting myself full-time to my Linotype machine. After all, I might not suffer so much if I got rid of these vague desires to become a writer.

As well, everyone around me agreed that *Contes gothiques* was a lousy title, that no publisher would read a manuscript with such a name. But no matter how hard I tried, I couldn't come up with anything better.

One night, in a little restaurant on Papineau Street near Sherbrooke, across from Parc Lafontaine, Brassard and Louise Jobin had for the first time given me a serious tongue-lashing and I'd come home feeling terribly let down: this time the terrible word "loser" had been pronounced. They hadn't told me that I was one, they didn't believe that yet, but they'd painted a grim enough picture of what lay ahead of me if I dropped everything; they'd alluded to the spectre of a wasted life, of a gnawing, undying regret that would inhabit me for the rest of my life, and as I listened to them, they were so convincing that I was already feeling the pinch of the remorse, the spite and the bitterness that lay in wait for me. Had they prepared their attack, or had it all come out that evening on its own, by chance, strictly out of friendship? I didn't know, but I was grateful to them for shaking me up, for provoking me to react.

Indeed, was I going to go on punching in at the print shop every night while they were making names for themselves in the history of Montreal theatre? Brassard was already gaining a reputation as a strange and arrogant young genius, people were starting to pay attention to some of the lesser individuals who surrounded him ... What could I tell them: that I was just a linotypist who'd wandered into the cultural crowd, that I was satisfied with running the boy wonder's fan club? My friends were right, I had to do something. Fast. It was becoming urgent. I was twenty-three years old, something had to happen before it was too late! I had to prove once and for all that I was somebody, even if I had serious doubts.

I had met Brassard several years earlier. We had been more than friends, we'd become inseparable partners who had the same thirst for culture, who read the same books, who raced to take in the same shows and films, with boundless enthusiasm and excitement. We let our enthusiasm be known when we liked something and we noisily displayed our discontent and contempt when we were let down. We went to the movies nearly every afternoon (I was working nights at the Imprimerie Judiciaire, from five p.m. till one a.m., the same schedule my father had followed over most of his life), André would sometimes walk me to work, pointing out ironically that the print shop smelled good but didn't lead anywhere ...

Now, through a happy coincidence the Imprimerie Judiciaire belonged to Les Éditions de l'Homme, which at the time was publishing the most popular, best-read books in Quebec. Also, the message from Louise and André was clear and increasingly insistent: why shouldn't I take advantage of being inside one of the biggest publishing houses in Quebec to get myself published? Maybe it could make things easier! I tended to think the opposite. For excellent reasons ...

I also have to say that I was the house weirdo at the Imprimerie Judiciaire. I'd been hired only because my brother Bernard had been working there for ages, it was a gift to him, a concession, and it didn't take them long to regret it. Not because I wasn't a good worker, I did a decent job, but because I was too different from the others, because I didn't mix with the homogeneous (and homo-phobic) group of workers, aristocrats of the working-class world who were waiting in vain for my submission and my oath of allegiance before they'd accept me within their bosom. But I worked nights—only two of us did—so they didn't really know me. In 1964, after the victory of *Le Train* and its television broadcast, they'd mocked, not congratulated, me and started calling me "the one-night wonder," which was particularly offensive because I thought pretty much the same thing ... I didn't really understand though why so much mockery for a colleague who, after all, had just won an big literary prize! Maybe they'd guessed that I was homo-sexual and had come up with that indirect way of rejecting me.

I hated being a linotypist. I think I'd chosen it during my third year at the Institute des Arts Graphiques to please my mother, who was concerned about my future, and because I knew it would soon disappear. Already I was allowing fate to decide on my life! And now, thirty years later, the profession hardly exists.

I had trapped myself: Mama had died right after I started at the Imprimerie Judiciaire and I was prisoner of a choice that made me a very well-paid worker but a desperately unhappy human being. Mama had been proud of me before she died because she thought my future was secure, but as far as I was concerned, I was facing a tunnel of which I couldn't see the end.

As the last linotypist hired by Imprimerie Judiciaire, I had of course been given the most boring, most repetitive job: every night I set the type for *Court House*, the court publication which, that's right! had an English name; I spent my evenings transforming into lines of lead the names of defendants and plaintiffs, addresses, telephone numbers, case numbers and codes of whose significance I had absolutely no idea. But sometimes, if *Court House* wasn't published or if there weren't enough sheets to copy, I got the chance to set on my linotype chapters of novels or guidebooks; it was very relaxing after the unbearably repetitive lists of *Court House*. For instance, that was how I became acquainted with Yves Thériault's novel *Agaguk*, which was being brought out for the first time in one volume, and I did a good part of the typesetting for the edition that's still available today ... I had quickly become a past master at copying the columns of figures in *Court House*, which the slightest moment's inattention could ruin, and I was always tense, nervous and anxious to be done, so I finished my work in a few hours and rarely made mistakes. When my half-hour meal break came, from ten till ten-thirty p.m., I had often finished my night's work and, to relax and pass the time, I'd go to the office of my boss, Noël Lespérance, and write. And that was how I'd produced all of *Les Belles-Soeurs*, between ten p.m. and one a.m. in August and September, 1965, by stealing time from the

Imprimerie Judiciaire. Without knowing it, I was the only Québécois author who was paid to write *while he was writing!*

And so I gathered my courage and in the fall of 1965, a few weeks after my conversation with Louise and André, I sent my manuscript to Les Éditions de l'Homme. I'd completely revised and corrected and, I hoped, improved my stories. I already had the habit of dating whatever I wrote; each tale bore a date between 1959 and 1962. The oldest were already six years old, which didn't look good, so I decided to "rejuvenate" my manuscript by moving as close as possible to 1965 the date on which I'd written them. (That inaccuracy wasn't corrected until the tales were brought out in paperback, in the mid-1980s.) Also, I nearly used a pseudonym so the publisher wouldn't know that it was an employee of the print shop who'd had the gall to send in the manuscript. But then I told myself that I had nothing to be ashamed of, that I ought to face up to my responsibilities and accept the consequences of my acts. So it was under my real name, typed in capitals and even underlined, that I submitted my so unGothic tales to the readers' committee of Les Éditions de l'Homme.

But I was lucky enough to be in a privileged position: as an employee working the night shift at Imprimerie Judiciaire, where the Éditions de l'Homme books were printed, bound and published, I had access to the offices and in a way I could chart the progress of my file. And so one evening I saw my *Contes gothiques* on the desk of Alain Stanké, the new director of the publishing house, under a pile of other recently received manuscripts. What emotion! But would he read it through to the end? Or put it aside after a few pages, thinking there was no fantastic literature in Quebec because no one was interested in it? Why bother publishing a book that was doomed in advance not to be read? And what if he came and threw it all in my face in the middle of *Court House*, laughing at my pretensions? In my paranoia I could already hear him shouting that I was a worker and that I ought to stay one!

I could take back my manuscript if I wanted, no one would know. It was right there on the desk, in the middle of other texts condemned to suffer the same fate, I just had to reach out my arm and take it ... Choose to stay in Brassard's shadow while continuing to earn a good living as a linotypist ... Remain an eternal neophyte ... A dilettante ... An *amateur*.

The temptation was strong but I resisted, thinking that in any event I wasn't risking anything, after all I hadn't signed it "Michel Tremblay, employee of Imprimerie Judiciaire, brother of Bernard Tremblay," and that the readers' committee wouldn't know where I worked and certainly had never heard of me; they would assess me objectively like any other writer. The worst that could happen, after all, was that they'd turn down my book. It would kill me, but at least I'd have tried and my friends would respect me when they buried me!

***

Months passed with no official word from Éditions de l'Homme. Every night I snooped around in Stanké's office, dreaming that I'd see my manuscript open on the publisher's desk, covered with appreciative remarks in red, like in school ... Or hoped not to find it because it had been sent to a specialist who would analyze it in depth, awed by my powerful imagination and my originality in writing a book in a genre hardly known in Quebec ... But it was still there, in the same place, in the middle of the pile of manuscripts, and in the end I assumed that they'd forgotten all about it. Or were acting as if they had. An undesirable they didn't know what to do with and had decided to leave there, in the hope that the author would realize he mustn't push it, that he had no talent and that some day, maybe, they'd sent it back to him.

Now and then I would see a manuscript sitting in Alain Stanké's out-basket. I'd pick it up, leaf through it. A rejection, polite but firm, always the same letter, was clipped to the title page, and I assumed that mine would eventually be returned to me in the same way.

Then I started noticing that they were talking about me behind my back at work again, that when I arrived to punch in at five minutes to five I was hearing again sarcastic remarks like I'd heard at the time of *Le Train*. They didn't look me in the eye, they'd say: "Salut, l'artiste!" winking and holding back laughter. So my manuscript had been read and word had got around. A bad sign.

Noël Lespérance, who came every afternoon to say hello to my work-mate Marcel and me, was red with embarrassment and I couldn't understand what he was jabbering. I wanted to say: "Let's forget it, give me back my manuscript so I can tear it up in front of you, if that's what you want; don't waste a stamp on me!" But I said nothing, nearly paralysed with embarrassment. I cleaned the little metal instruments that were used to make the spaces between words in the lines of lead, I leafed through the pages of *Court House* that I'd be copying that night, I gabbed with Marcel for a while, checked that I had enough molten lead in my machine to start my shift, the print shop emptied out, I started my linotype, sat down with despair in my heart and my stomach turning even though I hadn't eaten yet. Was this the end of my dream? My *Contes gothiques* turned down, *Les Belles-Soeurs* considered too vulgar to be produced ... I saw myself getting old in the heat and the smell of molten lead, I imagined myself a victim of lead poisoning, the linotypists' disease caused by inhaling lead salts, I put the first page of *Court House* in front of me: so-and-so of such-and-such address on such-and-such a date for such-and-such reason ... Agony!

***

The manuscript finally did come back one morning. The rejection letter was clipped to the title page as I'd predicted. Polite but firm. Very interesting, a great deal of imagination, but does not meet our publishing criteria. A little contempt, a hint of condescension, all in the cold style of a financier.

Panic.

Yet I'd been expecting this letter. The reaction of my fellow-workers and my foreman, their mockery, their insinuations (one day someone had muttered when he saw me walk in, "Hey, here comes Gothic!"), everything told me that my manuscript had been read and would be rejected. But somewhere inside me, buried deep in my soul, so deep that I wasn't aware of it, one last flame of hope must have been burning, a tiny vigil light that stayed on, enduring, after all the others had gone out one after another under the breath of disillusion. Every day that passed without my manuscript arriving in the mail represented twenty-four hours of hope gained over fate which, as I told myself after the mailman had gone, to give myself the courage to wait till the next day, maybe wasn't totally against me. Who knows, luck ...

I had many anxiety attacks before I could understand them, give them a name. In childhood, after a disappointment or bad news I would panic, my heart would feel as if it was sinking like a ship towards my solar plexus, I had trouble breathing, the present moment became absurd, impossible to live through—it was as if I were a spectator at what was happening to me rather than in control of my own life. Unable to control my emotions, without resources, a wreck. I threw myself into my bed and slept. Fortunately, I've always been able to take refuge in sleep. I still do but today, thanks to a miracle of modern science, a certain little pink pill quickly soothes my anxiety and I manage to function normally without feeling too powerful a need to escape through numbing sleep, while in the past all I could do was follow my instincts, dull my body and my pain, sometimes for very long periods.

That morning then I went to bed and slept like a log all day, only getting up to go to work. After all, I wasn't going to give them the pleasure of saying that I was sick! But what would happen when I got to the print shop? I pushed my paranoia to the point of imagining that everybody would be waiting to laugh at me (there was a reason why I wrote *Hosanna* six years later!) and that I'd collapse under the insults and mockery of my co-workers. None of which happened, of course. Faced with the panic, the despair that they must have seen on my face, they probably realized how important *Contes gothiques* was in my life and allowed me to make my way to my linotype, greeting me in a low voice. Noël Lespérance, probably uncomfortable, didn't come to say hello, the shop emptied quietly—so it seemed to me anyway—and I got through my night's work as usual.

But, surprisingly, at this period in my life when I rarely knew what I was doing and where I was going, I soon landed on my feet and retaliated in a way that I humbly admit was rather brilliant.

***

What do you do when a publisher turns down your manuscript? You send it to his competitor! And by chance the competitor of Alain Stanké at that time was Jacques Hébert, who had slammed the door of Les Éditions de l'Homme a few years earlier to start his own house, Les Éditions du Jour, which soon became the main breeding-ground of Québécois novelists: Victor-Lévy Beaulieu, Marie-Claire Blais, and André Major had already started their writing careers, and while Les Éditions du Jour wasn't as popular as the rival house, it was beginning to create an important place for itself in Québécois literature.

I got the address of Les Éditions du Jour from the phone book, attached to my manuscript an elegant letter addressed to Monsieur Hébert personally, in which I gave a rough account of my life story: I was a linotypist at Imprimerie Judiciaire, which he knew well, I had submitted my *Contes gothiques* to Les Éditions de l'Homme who, by rejecting it, were refusing to publish one of their own workers, though that would have been an interesting angle for publicizing the book, I was taking the liberty of sending him my tales so that he could tell me frankly what he thought of them—and so forth.

The response came quickly.

One morning a few weeks later, the phone rang. A pleasant secretary. Monsieur Jacques Hébert would like to meet me on such-and-such a day at such-and-such time, could I be there? Could I be there! Right away, if he wanted. In half an hour! No, no, such-and-such a day at such-and-such time, goodbye Monsieur Tremblay.

It had worked! I'd gambled on the rivalry between the two houses and I'd got an appointment with Jacques Hébert, the most important publishing figure in Quebec!

***

Les Éditions du Jour, on Saint-Denis Street, was a venerated sanctum where at any time you might meet the young lions of Québécois literature and the lions-in-waiting, more discreet and more reserved but with fire in their eyes and hope in their hearts. It was the nerve centre of our young literature, giving hope to the new writers wanting to win their spurs. I had once seen Marie-Claire Blais, frail, with brown bangs, climbing the short staircase with a manuscript under her arm; one afternoon I'd spotted Victor-Lévy Beaulieu, already impressive, reading a manuscript on the steps and fiddling with his beard. Now it was my turn to climb those steps, turn left onto the balcony that led to the front door, and I was so moved that I had trouble registering this important moment in my life. Had Victor-Lévy Beaulieu read my manuscript right here, in this beautiful old house not far from the Carré Saint-Louis, while he fiddled with his beard? If Les Éditions du Jour didn't publish my tales, at least I'd have been read by him and met the man in charge, which was infinitely better than a polite but firm letter ...

Jacques Hébert, his grey eyes scrutinizing me to the depths of my soul, obviously curious about the strange creature standing in front of him, got right to the point.

"Your letter amazed me. I had your manuscript read right away. Which also amazed us. Where do you come from? Nobody knows you. What are you doing at the Imprimerie Judiciaire?"

I told him everything: "science specialization" in high school because my marks were too high for me to take the normal courses, the Institut des arts graphiques because I didn't know what to do with my life if I didn't become a writer; the Imprimerie Judiciaire because my brother already worked there and I'd been hired without really taking a test; the Young Writers' Competition the year before, with a play I'd written seven years earlier—he had seen Le Train but didn't remember my name; and finally, these tales, written in the style of European and American fantasy writers, brought together under a title that, I assured him, wasn't definitive ...

"Glad to hear it! It's terrible, you'll have to change it."

"Change it ... Does that mean ... "

"Yes, we're interested in your book, but it needs work ... Not all your tales are good, you'll have to make a selection ... keep maybe thirty at most and find a theme for your book, try to bring them into line with each other ... Some are written in the first person, others not ... Try to group them, make a book with say two distinct parts, spend some more time on them, polish the style, which needs work ... But I'm giving you two weeks, no more, I want it out in June ... It's perfect holiday reading."

My own book! In June! In three months!

Jacques Hébert was obviously delighted by the pleasure that must have been obvious on my face.

"Are you going to give me a real contract and everything?"

"Yes. But our policy is to have new authors sign for five books ... That is, you sign a contract for this one but you give us first refusal rights for the next four ... We haven't had any complaints yet, and if you get to five ... "

"Don't worry, I've got a second one already!"

He was more and more surprised.

"A second one! More tales?"

"No, a play ... I finished it last September and ... "

He cut me off by raising both hands in front of him, waving them back and forth as if he'd just seen a ghost.

"Oh no, we aren't interested in theatre, not since our bad experience with Jean Basile's *Joli Tambour* ... "

"But it's really interesting, it's all about fifteen women pasting trading stamps in a kitchen ... "

"Don't push it, I don't even want to read it ... For a play, you'll have to go elsewhere ... We'll draft the contract accordingly ... "

"You might be sorry some day ... "

He looked me in the eyes while his smile disappeared.

"Don't make me sorry I've taken an interest in you, Michel ... And don't imagine that you're already a writer, don't quit your job yet, I'm telling you frankly, this is not the book that will let you earn your living as a writer! Keep working at Imprimerie Judiciaire or somewhere else, you've got a fine trade, I'm sure you earn a good living, later on we'll see if we can make a real writer out of you! I'll expect to hear from you in two weeks, no more, we have to reserve press time at the printer's ... "

I walked out of Les Éditions du Jour drunk as if I'd been drinking all afternoon. I walked down the Sherbrooke hill whistling blithely, my feet indifferent to the March shower that had got inside my Cossack boots which I'd started wearing too soon, as usual. I floundered about in the slush without a care in the world, without a thought for the winter that was lasting too long or the lousy late snowstorm that had hit us without warning ... My visit to Jacques Hébert was worth a cold!

I was meeting Brassard at the Sélect, at the corner of Saint-Denis and Sainte-Catherine. That very eclectic neighbourhood restaurant—the sign in the window that proclaimed *Canadian, Italian, Chinese, Continental Cuisine* said it all—was our dining hall, our rallying point, the place where we talked about the shows and movies we'd seen, the books we were reading; André met there with the actors and actresses he wanted to work with—it was there, two year earlier, that Rita Lafontaine and I had been officially introduced, a moment so important in my life that I could, I think, describe every second of it, every thousandth of a second!—we'd spend hours there over the remains of our good little low-priced meals—Brassard's hamburger platter with three gravies, no coleslaw, was famous—under the emotional looks of the waitresses whom we called "Mamma" or "Auntie." The jukebox served up non-stop, "C'est beau, la vie," by Jean Ferrat, and we had a good laugh at such inane optimism. Spread out in a booth that could hold six, making enough noise for twenty, we felt at home.

One by one or all at the same time, there were Louise Jobin, François Laplante, Ginette Lefebvre, Jean Archambault, Diane Arcand, Jacques Desnoyers, Micheline de Courval, Réjean Roy, Jean-Yves Laforce, the core group of artists or satellites like me with whom André had surrounded himself when he'd decided to start his own theatre company, Le Mouvement contemporain. Walking into a place and seeing faces light up at the sight of me was something new and precious; in recent years I'd got more used to indifference or to my co-workers' mockery when I turned up at work.

After the shouts of joy and the congratulations ("Fantastic! At last you're getting published!"), Brassard asked me to tell him all about my visit to Jacques Hébert.

But at the end of my story, which was full of detail, comments and a little bit amplified because I've always had a tendency to exaggerate, I finally expressed the last little concern that was gnawing at me:

"D'you think he's publishing me because he believes it's a good book or just to piss off Les Éditions de l'Homme?"

"You think he can afford to spend money just to piss off the competition?"

Relief. Laughter.

"Want another Coke? It's on me!"

***

When I walked into the Imprimerie Judiciaire that night I shouted very loud, loud enough to be heard at the back of the shop and inside the offices, by all the pressmen, linotypists, binders, the typographers, secretaries, proof-readers, Noël Lespérance, and Alain Stanké if he was there:

"My book's going to be published by Les Éditions du Jour!"

***

In less than a week I managed to restructure my tales, to sort them out, do some rewriting, and come up with the final title. I took Jacques Hébert's advice and separated out the stories told in the first person. Studying them closely, I soon realized that some, if they were assembled and linked together, could be like those Anglo-Saxon books in which old adventurers get together once a month to tell each other terrifying stories ... One, entitled "The Drunkard" as it happens, could serve as a conclusion to that part of the book.

I imagined some drinkers lingering in a sleazy tavern after closing time to confess to some terrible adventures they'd never dared to relate because they were afraid people would think they were crazy. There was a stench of stale beer and sweat. It was dark, the storytellers were sitting around a table ... They were talking sotto voce or shrieking in terror. I'd found my title: *Contes pour buveurs attardés* (Stories for Late Night Drinkers). In the first part, the drinkers speak; in the second, the author of the book tells them stories aimed at frightening them.

The book was better structured, the title infinitely better— even if my brother Jacques howled that you should never finish the title of a book with a past participle, that it wasn't proper French; in reply, I'd said, "You mean *À la recherche du temp perdu* is a bad title? Are you going to show Proust how to write?"—and I was jubilant when I went back to see Jacques Hébert.

With the final version dropped off at Les Éditions du Jour, the contract signed, the launch date set—it was, if I remember correctly, one of the first Mondays in June, 1966—now there was nothing to keep me at the Imprimerie Judiciaire, despite the wise admonitions of Jacques Hébert, and I started being frankly obnoxious at the shop. I arrived late, forgot to punch in, or took two hours to eat, asking Marcel to punch my card at ten and ten-thirty, I spent my evenings on the phone in Noël Lespérance's office; once I even showed up in a suit and tie because I was going to the theatre with Brassard at eight o'clock! My work got done though, the proofs of *Court House* were still left on the workbench when I left at one a.m. But the atmosphere there was becoming unbearable, I expected the worst and I didn't give a damn: my first book would soon come into the world and nothing else mattered.

One night when I was looking around for my brother Bernard's phone number in Noël Lespérance's office, because I wanted a gab with my sister-in-law, the foreman suddenly materialized like a comic strip hero, Superman defending the American way, Tarzan flushing out a monkey thief in Cheetah's nest, Blondie catching Dagwood with his head in the fridge.

I'd been expecting it for some time so I wasn't surprised. Someone had ratted on me, Noël, hiding somewhere, had been on the lookout ... It was all so ridiculous.

The explanation was long and painful. The foreman had good reason to chew me out and I let him go on without defending myself too hard. He poured his heart out and seemed relieved.

I lost my job, needless to say—this time Bernard couldn't cover for me—and that very night I left the Imprimerie Judiciaire where I'd spent the three worst years of my life.

As of that moment I was a writer, out of work like the others!

***

A few days before the launch, Jacques Hébert phoned to tell me that the book might not be delivered in time for the party.

"You know about printing problems, it's your field ... But don't worry, it's happened before and people tend to think it's funny."

"Not the author, I bet!"

"No, that's true, the author is often frustrated, but the book arrives the next day or a few days later and things get back to normal."

"What do you do at the launch party then? Pretend it's his birthday and sing 'Happy Birthday?'"

I was well aware that it wasn't his fault, but I was still furious. A book launch without a book! Like a première without a play! Or a wedding with no bride and groom!

It was my first book launch and it would be more like a funeral, with remorseful-looking guests and murmured conversations.

"Congratulations."

"For what?"

"What do you think? For your book!"

"Where is it?"

Honestly!

***

Like all book launches, mine was to start at five p.m. I was so nervous that day, I decided to go to the movies, to the first screening, to make the time pass more quickly. Don't even think of asking me what I saw, I have absolutely no memory, I doubt I could concentrate on what I was seeing. I came home around half-past three and washed and changed in fifteen minutes, leaving me an hour before I called for a taxi. I took a book onto the balcony.

It was a glorious June day, the rickety lilacs on de Lorimier Street were sending out their sugary perfume after a fashion, soon asphyxiated by the carbon monoxide from the thousands of trucks that drove past on their way to the Expo site. My father often remarked:

"We won't have to go to Expo, Expo drives right past our house every day!"

It was true that a fair amount of the earth used to build the islands for the Expo 67 site in the middle of the St. Lawrence came down de Lorimier Street day and night, making a horrible racket that had driven us crazy at first, but that over the years we'd finally got used to. Because it had been going on for years ... So Île Notre-Dame and La Ronde went past our place, one little pile at a time—yet another reason for disliking Mayor Jean Drapeau and his ideas of grandeur.

That day though the throbbing of motors being mauled by impatient drivers driven mad by the heat and humidity seemed worse than usual; I couldn't concentrate on my reading any more than I'd been able to concentrate on the movie I'd just seen, so I decided to walk down to Les Éditions du Jour. It would take a good half-hour, maybe a walk would relax me and I wouldn't get there too early. But if I did, it would give me a few minutes alone with my book ... That morning, Jacques Hébert had told me there was a chance that a few copies would arrive by bus ... One for me, one for him, a few for the press.

I remember very little about the route I took from de Lorimier near Masson down to Saint-Denis below Sherbrooke. It was as if I were in a deep coma from which I suspected I'd never emerge, from which I wasn't sure I *wanted* to emerge. I'd never been at a book launch in my life, I didn't have the faintest idea about what went on or what was expected of me. Would there be speeches like at an inauguration? Would I have to make a speech and thank Monsieur Hébert and take advantage of the moment to put down the despicable Éditions de l'Homme? Would my guests be there yet? Would they be able to get a copy of my book or would they have to share one copy that would pass from one to the next? Oh my God! I didn't have a pen on me! What if someone asked me to sign a book? The thought that I might have to write a dedication had never crossed my mind before and I nearly turned around to go home and hide in my bed.

All was quiet outside Les Éditions du Jour. It wasn't even a quarter to five. I'd come early to my own book launch like the nobodies, rather than turn up fashionably late! What was I going to do? Post myself at the front door like an old auntie who's giving a party and welcoming people as they arrive (if anyone did arrive, which I wasn't at all sure of).

"Hello ... Come in ... Thanks for coming ... Go right to the living room ... "

But then I told myself that Monsieur Hébert would help me, it was in his interest after all that I didn't seem too weird. I was arriving at my own book launch and it was only the third time I'd climbed the sacred staircase up to Les Éditions du Jour.

Just one person had got there before me. My friend Claire Sarrasin was standing in the front room, holding a book. I didn't pay any attention to the book but embraced Claire, telling her how glad I was she was there and that now I didn't feel all alone. She seemed moved and I swear that I didn't know why; in fact I wondered what was wrong with her.

Hugging the book, she said to me:

"It really looks good."

"What does?"

"The book, dummy!"

The book! It was there! And only then did I see the patches of blue and black on all the racks ... A tower, a clock showing five minutes to midnight, a hanged man clinging to the minute hand ...

Smiling, Claire held out her copy of *Contes pour buveurs attardés*. Everything around me faded away. I thought I was going to faint.

My first baby.

***

I love books, I've already said so often enough, I love to feel them, leaf through them, smell them; I love to hold them against me and bite them; I love to handle them roughly, feel them getting older in my hands, put coffee stains on them—though not deliberately—to smash small insects with them in the summer and to leave them around wherever they're liable to get dirty. But when I see one of my own books for the first time, a baby I've conceived, carried, delivered, my feelings are so much more powerful, the joy so much keener, that the earth practically stops turning. I feel a little jolt like when an elevator stops, my knees give way, my heart taps its feet as my Grandmother Tremblay used to do on the Fabre Street balcony when I was a child, and every time—the book you're holding now is number forty—I think about Mama who never knew that I was writing, whose death came too soon for two reasons: because I loved her, and because I was never able to confide the two secrets of my life to her: my sexual orientation and ...

What would she have said when she opened the first book by her son who'd exasperated her so often?

Let's imagine ...

"Michel! You wrote this book yourself! A hundred and eighty pages from your pen! After all the books I've read in my life, now I've given birth to a child who writes!"

"Mama, don't start thinking you wrote this one yourself!"

"I don't think I wrote it, all I said was I encouraged you to read and by encouraging you to read ... What's this, they've got some very odd titles, these stories of yours!"

"They're fantastic tales, Mama!"

"Fantastic tales?"

"Yes. Something like Edgar Allen Poe ... "

"Ah ... "

"I know you never liked this kind of story, but it's what I felt like writing."

"I see. But did you never feel like writing things that are, I don't know, maybe not so ... not so morbid?"

"Mama, you haven't even read them yet!"

"Maybe not but I know my genres! I suppose they're full of blood and killings and chopping-ups ... "

"Of course ... "

"And that's what you want me to read ... "

"Mama, they're stories that I wrote!"

"True enough. Mind you, it's a nice cover. Okay, listen, I'll give them a try ... "

"Try?"

"I'll read them, Michel. The whole book. To the very end. And I'll tell you right now, you'll know what I think!"

"You'll like it, Mama."

"Why'd you say that?"

"Because I'm the one who wrote them."

"True enough ... You have to make an effort in this life if you want to bring happiness to the people you love ... "

"Mama!"

"That was just a joke!"

"I'm not so sure ... "

"Now you listen to me, young man ... It's true I'll make an effort to like those stories of yours, even if I hate every word! But you'll never know because most likely I'll tell you it's the most wonderful book I've ever read in my life! To make you happy! To make *me* happy! You have to understand, it isn't possible that my child hasn't written the most wonderful book in the entire history of literature in the whole world!"

"I want you to be honest, Mama!"

"Buster, a mother is never honest!"

Key West, January 3–March 2, 1994